Mouth to Mouth

Mouth to Mouth

Poems by
Twelve Contemporary Mexican Women

Edited by
Forrest Gander

◆

Translated by

Zoe Anglesey, Lida Aronne-Amestoy, Martha Christina,
Brady Earnhart, Forrest Gander, Patricia Goedicke,
Jenny Goodman, Thomas Hoeksema, W. S. Merwin,
Janet Rodney, Stephen Tapscott, and C. D. Wright.

◆

With an introduction by
Julio Ortega

MILKWEED EDITIONS

MOUTH TO MOUTH

Printed in the United States of America.
Published in 1993 by Milkweed Editions.

Milkweed Editions
528 Hennepin Avenue, Suite 505
Minneapolis, Minnesota 55403
Books may be ordered from the above address.

ISBN 0-915943-71-9

93 94 95 96 97   5 4 3 2 1

First Edition

Publication of this book is made possible by grant support from the Literature Program of the National Endowment for the Arts, the Cowles Media / Star Tribune Foundation, the Dayton Hudson Foundation for Dayton's and Target Stores, Ecolab Foundation, the First Bank System Foundation, the General Mills Foundation, the Honeywell Foundation, the I. A. O'Shaughnessy Foundation, the Jerome Foundation, The McKnight Foundation, the Andrew W. Mellon Foundation, the Minnesota State Arts Board through an appropriation by the Minnesota State Legislature, the Northwest Area Foundation, the Lila Wallace-Reader's Digest Literary Publishers Marketing Development Program, and by the support of generous individuals.

Library of Congress Cataloging-in-Publication Data

Mouth to mouth : poems by twelve contemporary Mexican women /
    edited by Forrest Gander ; translated by Lida Aronne-Amestoy . . .
    [et al.] ; with an introduction by Julio Ortega.
        p.   cm.
    ISBN 0-915943-71-9
    1. Mexican poetry – Women authors.   2. Mexican poetry – 20th
century.   3. Mexican poetry – Translations into English.   I. Gander,
Forrest, 1956–   .
PQ7253.M68   1993
861—dc20   92-18246
                                                            CIP

This book is dedicated to my parents,
Ruth and Walter Gander.

Acknowledgments

The editor gratefully acknowledges the invaluable assistance of: Susan Brown, Rocio Aragon, Pilar Coover, Anne Hohenstein, Sylvia Madrigal, Ken Clauser, Ellen Conroy, Tony Nunes, and especially Jason Weiss, whose fine translations of Enriqueta Ochoa were omitted from the final anthology. The Rhode Island State Council for the Arts helped to support this project; so did Providence College in the form of a CAFRA grant to the editor.

Translations of Coral Bracho by Thomas Hoeksema were first published by *Mid-American Review;* Hoeksema's translations of Isabel Fraire appeared in *Poems in the Lap of Death* (Latin American Literary Review Press) and in *Poems* (Mundus Artium).

The following Spanish poems in *Mouth to Mouth* were originally published in these Spanish editions:

Carmen Boullosa, *El hilo olvida:* "Dark Water," "The Figure," "Light and Shadow."

Coral Bracho, *El ser que va a morir:* "A Lightning Bug under the Tongue," "Distant Cities," "I Refract Your Life Like an Enigma," "Their Decorated Eyes of Crystalline Sand," "Your Borders: Crevices That Uncover Me," "*Your voice. . . .*"

Elsa Cross, *Canto Malabar:* Parts III and IV.

Isabel Fraire, *Poemas en el regazo de la muerte:* "A Moment Captured by a Japanese Painter," "Housing Complex," "*the minute the sun comes out . . . ,*" "Noon," "*time. . . .*"

Kyra Galván, *Un pequeno moreton en la piel de nadie:* "Bellas Artes," "City Woman," "Conversation with Emily Dickinson," "Debris of Song," "Why Life Runs On and Does Not Happen."

Gloria Gervitz, *Shajarit:* "*In the migrations of red carnations. . . .*"

Gloria Gervitz, *Yiskor:* excerpts.

Elva Macías, *Circulo del Sueno:* "Nostalgia," "Stanzas," "The Steps of the One Who Comes."

Elva Macías, *Imagen y Semejanza:* "Hansel and Gretel," "Image and Likeness."

Mónica Mansour, *Con la vida al hombro: "a man is staring at a woman . . . ," "Cenote . . . ," "Convent . . . ," "downcast eyes . . . ," "there are mountains here . . . ," "this black telephone. . . . "*

Mónica Mansour, *Desnudo (Aguafuerte): "I don't know whether I miss you . . . ," "Look, honey, you don't know me. . . . "*

Elena Milán, *Corredor Secreto:* "Dinosaur Heart," "Face to Face," "Folklore," "Hallucination I," "Relentless Pursuit," "Trip South," "Word Puzzle I."

Myriam Moscona, *Ultimo Jardin:* "Auschwitz Garden," "Garden of Beasts," "Last Garden," "Lost Garden," "Lot's Wife Is Nameless," "Lot's Wife Takes a Name," excerpt from "Garden in Peril": Part II.

Silvia Tomasa Rivera, *Apuntes de Abril:* "From the Coastal Road," *"When it rains in the south. . . . "*

Silvia Tomasa Rivera, *Poemas al desconocido/poemas a la desconocida: "From the midnight of my room . . . ," "I'd give anything to know . . . ," "I'll be whatever you want . . . ," "What I feel for you. . . . "*

Verónica Volkow, *Litoral de Tinta:* "Self-Portrait, Dead," "The Washerwoman," "The Weariness of Eurylochus."

Verónica Volkow, *El Inicio:* Parts I, VI, X, and XI.

Mouth to Mouth

Introduction

On October 2, 1968, the Mexican army assaulted the Tlatelolco Plaza and killed several hundred demonstrating students. The massacre put an end to the student protest movement and its demand for greater democracy in Mexican society. On September 19, 1985, Mexico suffered another catastrophe no less devastating: the earthquake that destroyed much of the capital city, killed and maimed hundreds, and left thousands homeless. Between one catastrophe and the other, a history describing itself in cycles of tragic self-revelation, everything changed in Mexico. A true social mobilization, supported by a wide base of organizations, soon began to dominate the political spectrum, challenging the system and prodding it to open up. From the street protests of students to the organized resistance of women workers, the popular push for a more participatory government gained momentum. Democratic experience came to be viewed as a critical exercise in community reconstruction. In few parts of the world have we seen a people convert disaster into political opportunity. A tragic learning experience thus produced a historical one.

Still, we cannot know the extent to which Mexican society has changed or will change between one test of the system's limits and another, but we can recognize how drastically Mexican literature has been altered, and along with it society's cultural conscience. Hence the diversity of subjects—and treatments of the same—portraying a torn, modern Mexico. It is not by chance that we owe the first literary accounts of both catastrophes to Elena Poniatowska, a writer and social critic whose work, by engaging a feminine discourse, threatened much of the patriarchal literary canon. From the intimate stories of the victims and from the witnesses of both tragedies, Poniatowska constructed true social frescoes (*La noche de Tlatelolco* in 1969 and *Nadie, nada* in 1986) in which we can see the spirit of people touched by the urgency of their own self-revelation, see it in the shattered mirror of their immediate experience. Extraordinarily, that spirit manifested itself in the discovery of a community identity in which a specific and lucid speech emerged, one which reconstructed—by reinventing—the subject of the world. From the ruins of the apocalypse arose the protagonists of a new foundation. In this living fresco, like those painted by Diego Rivera,

we see a communitarian subject capable of surpassing all previous
classifications for defining it.

Exploring other metaphors for the crisis and other strata of interaction,
numerous Mexican writers have turned to autobiographical forms. Already,
Sor Juana de la Cruz, the major Hispanic poet of colonial times and even
today an intriguing emblem of feminine discourse, demonstrated that
biographical rhetoric could be a protean literary form for women. For
writers like Elena Garro and Rosario Castellanos to construct a narrative of
the feminine subject, they had to reinvent the familiar autobiographical
chronicle. The result was a tribal story. In their respective major Latin
American epics (*Memorias del porvenir* and *Oficio de tinieblas*), Garro and
Castellanos improved upon allegory by employing intricate family stories.
They felt the need to transcend a formal expression that did not account
sufficiently for the heterogeneous reality of society. Garro, in theater as
well as in her novels, and Castellanos, in journalism, poetry, and novels,
together confronted the desperation of the time, the decade of the fifties,
with an admirable, intellectual passion. More independently, and without
critical appreciation, Ines Arredondo (1929-1989), who is one of the best
and one of the most disturbing modern Mexican writers, dedicated herself
to exposing her culture's malaise, its perturbation and bewilderment.
Rio subterraneo (1967), her most important book, seems to have pushed
autobiography into stammer; she extirpated autobiography's digressive
eloquence in order to reseed the form with profound questioning. Among
the younger writers, Carmen Boullosa (*Antes*) has introduced irony to an
autobiographical address that is not a hyperbole of the feminine "I," but
that turns out to be a phantasmic tale: she narrates from her Death, as if a
woman could not be represented, after all, except by her own absence and
by the oppositional utterance of a fragmentary narrative. So it is that
Margo Glantz, in her parodic reformulation of the first-person narrative,
proposes that "genealogies" are social and biographical chronicles that
divulge their authors' biases as well as their purported values.

On the one hand, in Mexican literature we rely upon the device of
immediate testimonials that present images of women in their urgent,
critical, and refractory daily lives. This type of writing was pioneered by
Elena Poniatowska, who, by conjoining fictive and journalistic techniques,
exposed the popular construction of objectivity, a literary point of view

that contemporary Mexican women have taken a decisive role in developing. More recently, Cristina Pacheco has applied this method to stories told in the plainest speech, making journalism a creative instrument with which to listen to and transcribe the voices of the poorest of the poor, the voices of women beyond the margin, to reveal the most fragile—and at the same time the most resistant—part of the social web.

On the other hand, the representation of the marginal feminine subject is achieved through a narration displaced from the canon, one that actually subverts the traditional rhetorical structures, thereby deconstructing its very subjects. This feminine discourse of "no-identity" begins to dissolve the adversarial limits of genres in the institution of the literary—and in the institutionalization of the social—structure. From the work of Ines Arredondo to the recent novels of Carmen Boullosa, this practice unmasks the specificity of the voices of women whose differences describe a "no-place" of speech, a fissure in speaking.

The borders of contemporary Mexican literature have expanded since its women writers have advanced with their own intonations, dimensions, and demands. This is true of several Latin American countries—especially Argentina, Uruguay, Chile, and Venezuela—where these new works posit a crisis in the dominant expressive tradition. Simply put, women have radicalized writing by articulating the processes of democratization and cultural resistance.

One of the best examples of the ongoing breakthroughs in literary activity is this anthology of contemporary Mexican poets. It is significant that the first poet, **Silvia Tomasa Rivera,** writes as if she were another: "I'm someone else now," she says midway through one poem. And this "other" is the revelatory voice of her sexuality as a woman. Her lambent, amorous dialogue flows from images of fertility to promise, and surges toward the mature lyricism of a desire that conjugates words and flesh in a new order.

Mónica Mansour looks at erotic dialogue not for the miracle of the senses but for the meaning of the miracle. In one of her best poems, she responds to César Vallejo, rewriting from her perspective one of the few love poems by the great Peruvian poet. It is not so much the style as the point of view—the partner's testimony—that transforms the Vallejo.

Carmen Boullosa enters and exits poetry as if its generic boundaries were the most natural space for her writing. Her poetry presents itself as the document of these border excursions, where elements of the world are recomposed by syntax and where the subject is denoted by a discourse that precedes yet does not explain it. In such a way, poetry is not an a posteriori exercise but the rehearsal of a search, a fragmentary grappling with the indeterminacy of our being here with no more proof than these words which are heard, read, assumed.

Kyra Galván is likewise critical; however, in her poems she attempts to make of the urban experience a legitimate, human space for dialogue. Recent immigrants stand out in her poems as the presence of the "other," an other who demands to be a part of our own identity. With a discontinuously narrative form, Galván weaves together fragments of story. Her soliloquies have a flexible, colloquial texture. In "Conversation with Emily Dickinson," she displays her capacity for reflexive self-irony, that game of mirrors in which the poem is positioned incisively against a normative discourse.

The ironic imagination of **Elena Milán** assembles probable settings by which the poem can assume the countenance of a critical fable, and this antilyrical activity appropriately emphasizes that poetic language is capable of more than simple expression. The poem dedicated to Alaide Foppa, the Guatemalan writer exiled in Mexico who disappeared when she revisited her country, states it explicitly: hers is the "early dawn voice to begin a story." To tell this story, the poem must speak a new language of imprecation; it simply cannot be conciliatory. It must be an instrument of both discrepancy and affiliation.

In her part, **Gloria Gervitz** positions herself within the Semitic poetic tradition of the psalms, accounts of wonders in the exuberant world. But she quickly introduces into this celebration of fullness the unresolved question of the woman as subject, detached from and doubtful of her own identity. She writes the tale of her nomadic marginality, where her voice is her footprint. "We are what moves," she writes, and her poems are the track of the enigma.

Isabel Fraire employs notably distinctive forms, riveting into her poems fragments of astonishment and awe. Her work is concerned with annotating possibilities, and even when her poem becomes a utopian declaration, it forces us first to confront the long detour, the detour that—in a jolt of revelation—we recognize as the new road.

Another tradition is proclaimed in the poetry of **Elsa Cross,** a poet who seeks to transcend personal experience through philosophical and meta-physical concentration, a project already at the edge of literature. Her precise, enumerative writing communicates the fullness of the moment in a world that is harmonious but evanescent. It translates the account of a miraculous dialogue that the poem registers as a substitution ritual, the words superseding and choosing their speaker. The reflective mood of the work suggests as well the yearning for a sacred speech.

On a different track, **Verónica Volkow,** in "Self-Portrait, Dead," obscures the protagonistic role of the meditative subject. She introduces the purifying possibilities of negation, a negative cosmos. But the blackness of that cosmos is another ink; from ashes and still glowing "coals," the poet will rekindle the flames of the whole word again. This same ritual sensi-bility distinguishes the vehemence of Volkow's erotic poetry, which pulses, setting loose and rebinding its characters.

Myriam Moscona's dramatic sense of irony permits her to distance herself from her poems' characters in order to suggest a critical point of view. She also maintains an uncommon capacity for precisely narrowing the foci of her poems to eloquent, vigorous images.

Among these poets, **Coral Bracho** has carried furthest an exploration of the poem in open forms, in several layers, prompting abundant permuta-tions. In one way, her poems seem to take place as patterns in space, patterns interposed by allusions and expansions. Then again, her poems do not dissolve into other forms of speech but concentrate within themselves the activity of renaming the meditative subject—the finger, eye, and mouth, each of which is a single instrument for summoning, varying, and displacing the poem's verbal and material history in a rich, circular prosody. As such, she manages—by the greatest density of discursiveness—to arouse the sensorial, the ceremonial.

—Julio Ortega
Brown University

Silvia Tomasa Rivera

Silvia Tomasa Rivera was born in El Higo, Veracruz, on March 7, 1956. Her first two books, *Duelo de espadas* and *Poemas al desconocido/poemas a la desconocida,* both published in 1984, describe a rural life, Rivera's childhood in the countryside, and love's multiple passions. *Apuntes de abril*, published by Universidad Veracruzana in 1986, is Rivera's most recent book, and it has been described as "an existential exercise in locating the nature of all things sexual."

◆

The town where I was born is situated in the north of the state of Veracruz; nearby there is a river on whose banks I began to write my first poems. During my childhood, I lived on my parents' ranch, a few kilometers from town, and I would write while looking out at the hills. At the age of eighteen, I arrived in Mexico City with a book of verse. My road has been difficult; to survive I have had to take jobs that had nothing to do with poetic sensibility. But the satisfaction of publishing my work has no price.

POR EL CAMINO DEL MAR LLEGAN
LOS HOMBRES

Por el camino del mar llegan los hombres
a esperar el alza de la luna.
Afortunados, el mar rejuvenece.
En este viego puerto, la sal carcome el caserío
de madera labrada.

Ellos vienen a olvidarse de sí,
traen cervezas, cigarros y el deseo
para gastarlo a tientas.
Hay emoción ritual,
el cíclico verano incuba huevos.
Esperan, olfatean, preparan el inicio.

Llena la luna irrumpe.
Nutrida está de sangre.

Los hombres ¿son lobos o son dioses?
Y si son dioses
¿por qué aúllan cuando se abre la noche?

FROM THE COASTAL ROAD

Men arrive from the coastal road
to await the ascension of the moon.
Fortune's darlings, the sea makes them young again.
In this old port, salt consumes
the wood-hewn village.

They come separately to forget themselves
carrying beer, cigarettes and the desire
to spend at random.
There is ritual emotion,
the cyclical summer heats up their balls.
They wait, they sniff, they prepare their come-ons.

The full moon erupts.
Nourished by blood.

The men, are they wolves or gods?
And if they are gods
why do they howl when the night looms open?

Translated by Zoe Anglesey

SIN TÍTULO

—*a M. A. G.*

Lo que siento por tí,
no persigue ningún fin rebuscado en el ocio;
es tan simple como las cosas que componen el mundo,
como ir al mercado,
como ver a los amantes peleando a la entrada de un cine,
como hacer el amor en un cuarto de azotea
mientras pasa la lluvia.
Lo que siento por tí,
no alcanza a romper los vidrios cuando me emborracho.
No me orilla a mentarte la madre si no llegas
ni a ponerme celosa de la rubia
que causa conmoción con su pestañas.
Es algo más sencillo,
como abrir la ventana y palpar esa mancha luminosa
                                            que revienta en tus manos.

UNTITLED

—to M. A. G.

What I feel for you
has no pursuits or gain gleaned in idleness;
it's as simple as worldly things
like going to market,
like seeing a lovers' quarrel at the movies,
like making love in an attic room
until the rain stops.
What I feel for you
doesn't quite shatter the windows when I'm drunk.
Doesn't make me call your mother names if you don't come
or arouse my jealousy of the blonde
whose eyelashes cause a stir.
It's something much simpler,
like opening a window and touching that luminous spot
                             bursting in the cup of your hands.

Translated by Janet Rodney

SIN TÍTULO

Desde la medianoche de mi cuarto
te conjuro
—hombre de medianos conflictos—
y te exhorto a que te vistas
de vida.
No intentes acostumbrarme
a tus desprecios
no quiero atraparte
entre mis redes
(ni que fueras monstruo marino).
Lo que sí me gustaría
es jugar con tus barbas más seguido
y hacer figuritas en tu cuerpo
con mi lengua de víbora.
Puedes estar tranquilo
tampoco pretendo
hacer un río subterráneo
con la última gota
de tu semen.
Sólo pido un lugar
junto a tu cuerpo
algunas veces
en este invierno
y después—lo prometo—
regresarte a la muerte.

UNTITLED

From the midnight of my room
I conjure you
—oh man of middling concerns—
I exhort you to put on
the cloak of life.
Don't try to get me used to
your scorn
I'm not after you
with my nets
(not even were you a monster of the deep).
What I would like
is to play a little more with your beard
and make patterns on your body
with my serpent tongue.
You can rest assured
I'm not plotting
an underground river
with your last drop of semen.
All I ask is for
a place next to your body
a few times
to warm me
and then—I promise—
I'll return you to the dead.

Translated by Janet Rodney

SIN TÍTULO

Qué diera yo por saber
                qué hago aquí
sobre este raído sofá, masturbándome,
                con un amante ausente
que me pega—y que amo.
En la calle es lo mismo.
Me duelen los hombres que me dicen
alguna palabra creyendo que es obscena,
son como pájaros heridos que se estrellan
en una ventana sin cristal.
Soy mujer fuera de época.
Justo cuando deseaba ser locamente amada
por un estibador, o revolcarme con un asesino
sobre un costal de papas, decido guardar mi sexo,
mis pechos, mis cabellos, en un cuarto a medialuna,
y salir con la pura alma a corretear gorriones.

UNTITLED

I'd give anything to know
              what I'm doing here
masturbating on this worn-out sofa
              with an absent lover
who is beating me—and whom I love.
In the street it's the same.
I feel sorry for men who whisper to me
what they think is a dirty word,
they are like wounded birds
smashing against glassless windows
I am a woman of another era.
Just when I wanted to be madly loved
by a docker, or to cavort with a killer
over a bag of potato chips, I decide to
lock away in a moonlit room
my breasts, my hair, my sex
and go out pure soul to chase sparrows.

Translated by Janet Rodney

SIN TÍTULO

Seré lo que tú quieras
cuando las hojas caigan.
La adivina seré detrás de la ventana.
Cuando llegues, no pensaremos más,
nada extrañaremos,
bastará la luz de nuestros cuerpos.
Para que se iluminen los paisajes.

Las rosas, las caprichosas
se han secado,
los pétalos están ahora en tí
y yo juego con ellos.

UNTITLED

I'll be whatever you want
when the leaves fall.
I'll be the fortune-teller behind the window.
When you come, we won't think anymore,
we will lack for nothing,
our body-light will suffice
to illuminate the landscape.

The roses, stubborn things,
have dried up,
the petals are in you
and I am playing with them.

Translated by Janet Rodney

SIN TÍTULO

Esta tarde pasadas las 6
habré muerto,
no te llamaré más de madrugada
mientras reposas con una mano débil sobre el sexo.

No me sabrás mañana
buscando tu costado
con los cabellos revueltos
en horas de oficina.

Esta tarde pasadas las 6
no más disculpas,
habré muerto de veras;
será una muerte limpia,
a prueba de domingos y de insomnio.
Ni una gota de alcohol habrá en la duda.

Esta tarde, pasadas las 6
yo espero
para aclarar los puntos de esta muerte
y anochecer segura, tocando las estrellas.

UNTITLED

A little after 6 this evening
I will have died.
I won't call you anymore
in the middle of the night
while you lie with a weak hand on your sex.

You won't taste me tomorrow
when you feel at your side
with your hair messed up
during office hours.

A little after 6 this evening
no more excuses.
I will have really died;
it will be a limp death,
Sunday- and insomnia-proof.
Not a drop of alcohol in my doubt.

A little after 6 this evening
I'll be waiting for you
to clear up the details of this death
so I can rest easily, touching the stars.

Translated by Brady Earnhart

SIN TÍTULO

Corro hacia el jardín,
mis pies desnudos extrañan la grama
del lugar donde nací, chocan con el cesped,
machacan vidrios y mi sangre forma
extrañas figuras sobre los adoquines.
Ahora soy otra.
Entro en la fuente,
suelto mis cabellos,
el mar es un sonido agudo
repiqueteando en el cerebro.
La noche es mi verdad.
Tras el farol,
un muchacho moreno me observa,
su mirada tiene el brillo de una espiga
en tiempos de lluvia.

UNTITLED

I run for the garden,
my bare feet yearn for the grass
of the place I was born, they slide in the lawn,
crush bits of glass and my blood falls
in strange patterns on the walk.
I'm someone else now.
I go into the fountain,
my hair down,
the sea is a sharp clanging in my brain.
The night is my truth.
From behind the lamppost
a dark-skinned boy is observing me,
his look has the glint of an ear of corn
in times of rain.

Translated by Brady Earnhart

SIN TÍTULO

Cuando llueve en el sur
lo de menos son las aguasnegras
                que se encharcan.

Una pinta sostiene la pared:
"ciega estoy perdida de tus ojos".
La pareja debajo de un paraguas
dice que aún se puede, que no son ciertos
los nubarrones de los días que vienen.
Santo Domingo respira el aroma húmedo
de los pedregales.
7 p.m. ¿Dónde dejaste la cerveza?
La calle tiene una limpieza ofensiva.

Hay que perderse siempre, buscar refugio
bajo la piedra negra del volcán.
¿Y el horizonte, hasta qué punto veremos
                el horizonte?

12 p.m. hora de la *razzia*.
¿No han llegado los otros,
                no existirá tu espalda?

UNTITLED

When it rains in the south
black waters that pool
                are the least of it.

The wall bears a graffiti:
"Away from your eyes I am blind."
The couple under an umbrella
says oh yes we can, and the clouds
of days to come are not real.
Santo Domingo breathes the wet smell
of stony fields.
7 P.M. Where did you put the beer?
The street is offensively clean.

You've always got to get lost, seek shelter
under the black volcanic rock.
And the horizon, to what extent will we be able
                to see the horizon?

12 P.M., the looting hour.
The others aren't here yet, does that mean
                your back isn't real?

Translated by Janet Rodney

▼▼▼

Mónica Mansour

Mónica Mansour was born in Buenos Aires, Argentina, in 1946 and has
lived in Mexico since 1954; she is a divorced mother of three children. A
writer, literary critic, and translator, she received her master's degree in
Iberoamerican letters at the National Autonomous University of Mexico.
She has published several studies on contemporary Hispanic writers. Among
her books of poetry are *Silencios de tierra y otros arboles* (1981), *Desnudo
(Aguafuerte)* (1983), *Con la vida al hombro* (1985), and *Vertigo* (1990). In
addition, she has published a book of short stories, *Mala memoria* (1984),
and a book of "tales" in collaboration with Maria Luisa Puga (1986).
Formerly a professor, Mansour has dedicated herself principally to research
and translation.

◆

*They often ask of one's influences, and I think that influences are total: all
circumstances, all people, all readings. Everything influences us. Nevertheless, I will
mention the authors that I re-read the most: Vallejo, Sabines, Jamis, Eliot, Rulfo,
Del Paso.*

*Erotic poetry written by women is, perhaps, what best shows a radical change of
contemporary attitudes. In the first place, it is a change in regard to literature: the
theme of eroticism was absolutely prohibited for women. In the second place, and
above all, it reflects a change in life and society. We women have healed our bodies
and all that we experience through them: this is expressed to a large degree in our
poetry, be it erotic or not. Poetry written by women tends to be sensual.*

SIN TÍTULO

convento
lleno de ruidos y humedad
no hay música
esperamos
al pie del tepozteco
esperamos el silencio
para decir un pedazo de vida
tantos hombres y mujeres
no sabemos descifrar tus escollos
aquí están todos los dioses de la historia

tepozteco y convento de misterios
dioses hombres mujeres reunidos
para decir sólo un pedazo de vida
en estas pocas palabras
en esta espera del silencio
perfecto

(Tepoztlán, octubre de 1984)

UNTITLED

convent
full of sounds and humid air
there is no music
we wait
at the foot of tepozteco
we wait for the silence
to say a bit about life
so many men and women
don't know to decipher your coral reefs
here are all the deities of history

tepozteco and convent of mysteries
deities men women convened
to say only a bit about life
in these few words
in this wait of perfect
silence

(Tepoztlán, north of Mexico City, October of 1984)

Translated by Zoe Anglesey

SIN TÍTULO

cenote
agua serenada
las raíces se disparan desde un lecho
para alcanzar el azul del cielo
y se enredan en las ramas del árbol más próximo
tus bocas respiran aire de mundo
dos rayos de luz se disparan desde el azul
hacia la oscuridad de tus piedras reposadas
y se quedan pegados al agua

atravieso tu rostro sereno inpenetrable
la frescura que no prestas al sol
y así sé de tus venas en la tierra
donde corre el sufrimiento de la historia
bajo nuestros pasos pesados

penetro tu serenidad
luego me cubre el sol

(Dzidzantún, Yucatan)

UNTITLED

cenote
tranquil water
roots dart from the riverbed
to reach the blue of sky
and tangle in branches of the closest tree
your mouths breathe in the planetary air
twin rays of light fire from the blue
toward the dark shade of your solemn stones
and they stay wedded to water

I move across your serene impenetrable face
the coolness you do not render to the sun
and so I learn of your veins in the earth
where the sufferings of history course
under our heavy footsteps

I disturb your composure
then the sun ignites me

(Dzidzantún, Yucatan)

Translated by Zoe Anglesey

SIN TÍTULO

se avergüenzan los ojos
entre las tierras calcinadas
una luz tibia corta el aire
bocas de piedra bajo el sol

se avergüenzan los ojos
cuando se alza la tierra hacia el día
escapando el salitre
se alza a tientas por la piel
buscando la saliva

entonces hay que caminar despacio
es tanto lo que pesa esta tierra
bajo los pies

(Matehuala)

UNTITLED

downcast eyes
between charred plains
a faint light cuts the air
the mouths of stone under the sun

downcast eyes
when the earth rises up toward the day
escaping the salty rock
when it rises up groping along the skin
in want of saliva

then there is the slow walk
this earth weighs so much
under our feet

(Matehuala, central Mexico)

Translated by Zoe Anglesey

SIN TÍTULO

hay montañas aquí
de esas montañas que andan
pisoteando la tierra
y dejan huella   no sé

hay valles y ríos   mares
y cielos   selvas y manglares
que caen para renacer
entre lo profundo
        y todo es hermoso

pero el aire golpea
desde la siembra hasta las calles
el ruido retumba   no sé
dice hambre
o dice hombre
dice sangre no derramada
sino a punto de hervir

no sé
en la montaña suceden
estas cosas

(Nayarit)

UNTITLED

there are mountains here
I don't know about those mountains that amble
trampling the earth
to leave no tracks

there are valleys and rivers   seas
and skies   *selvas* and stands of mangrove
that fall to reseed
between what's deep
        and every beautiful thing

but the winds blow
from cultivated fields to city streets
I don't know if the resounding roar
says hunger
says humanity
says blood doesn't spill
except at the boiling point

I don't know
in the mountains
these things happen

(*Nayarit, west coast*)

Translated by Zoe Anglesey

SIN TÍTULO

No sé bien si te extraño. No sé bien si ésta es una historia de amor. Cuando me caía encima el velo, sabes, levanté los brazos. Y después los bajé, pero el velo quedó enredado en un ala de pájaro. Por eso, si miro para arriba me envuelve, pero si miro de frente sólo están allí los árboles desaliñados en forma de bosque.

UNTITLED

I'm not sure whether I send you packing. I'm not really sure if this is love's chronicle. When the veil was drawn over me, I raised my arms. And later, I let them fall, but the veil tangled in a bird's wing. So that now, if I look up, it shrouds me, but if I look straight ahead, I see trees strewn in the shape of a forest.

Translated by Forrest Gander

SIN TÍTULO

Mire, compañero, usted no me conoce, ni yo lo conzco a usted. Por eso nunca lo recuerdo: sólo algunos detalles de libertad o algunos de ternura. Porque, sabe compañero, cuando pasamos varios días juntos, los ocupamos en darnos esos detalles que hacen falta para la vida cotidiana, día con día. Por eso sólo recuerdo los detalles; lo demás, sabe, ni lo conozco.

UNTITLED

Look, friend, you don't know me, and I don't know you. I can't make out
that much: only a few details of liberation and some of tenderness.
Because, you know, when we spend several days together, we spend them
feeding ourselves those details necessary for life as it is lived day by day.
As far as that goes, I remember the details; the rest, you understand, I
cannot fathom.

Translated by Forrest Gander

SIN TÍTULO

este teléfono negro
anchos hombros cabeza gacha
te permite entrar en mí
sin llave ni ganzúa
sin invitación
y de pronto se llena de silencios
yo me quedo esperando la voz
tu voz que trata de entender
la ventana el sillón la mesa el sol
adentro de esta casa

UNTITLED

this black telephone
shouldering a lowered head
permits you access to me
without key or lock pick
without invitation
and suddenly it fills with pauses
I'm left waiting for the voice
your voice which would fathom
the window, the armchair, the table, the sun
inside this house

Translated by Forrest Gander

▼▼

SIN TÍTULO

un hombre está mirando a una mujer
está mirándola inmediatamente
               —César Vallejo

"un hombre está mirando a una mujer
está mirándola inmediatamente":
es testigo el poeta
(inmediatamente la mujer giró
en movimiento abierto)
una mujer está abrazando una mirada
está abrazándola irremediablemente:
es testigo el silencio
(irremediablemente la mirada habló
en cuerpo extenso)
una mirada está tocando una palabra
está tocándola repentinamente:
es testigo el hombre
(repentinamente el hombre retiró
su palabra inmediata)
pero junto a su silencio
queda la tierra última del rumor:
es testigo el poeta

UNTITLED

> a man is staring at a woman
> immediately staring at her
> —*César Vallejo*

"a man is staring at a woman
immediately staring at her":
the poet bears witness
(immediately the woman pirouetted
openly)
a woman embraces a stare
irremediably embracing it:
the silence bears witness
(irremediably the stare spoke
its generous body)
a stare is caressing a word
suddenly caressing it:
the man bears witness
(suddenly the man took back
his immediate word)
but next to his silence
the borrowed landscape of rumor continues:
the poet bears witness

Translated by Forrest Gander

Carmen Boullosa

Carmen Boullosa was born in Mexico City in 1954. Her first book, *El hilo olvida*, was published in 1978. Since then she has published a number of books of poetry, including *Abierta* (1983), *Lealtad* (1981), and *La salvaja* (1989); as well as fiction, *Mejor desaparece* (1987), *Antes* (1989), *Son Vacas, Somos Puercos* (1991); and children's stories. Boullosa has also worked in the theater, writing and adapting plays which have been performed throughout Mexico. In 1989 she was awarded the Premio Xavier Villaurrutia.

◆

I was born in 1954, raised by a Christian family and educated by Ursuline Sisters. Clearly not for writing. The story I consider valid is that I formed myself from the moment I decided I was a writer (because I never asked myself if I could be one or whether writing was my vocation). Curiously enough, now that I am a writer the majority of my themes come from my "pre-history," from my childhood, my puberty, my brothers and sisters, my childhood companions.

*As a writer, I don't limit myself to thinking I am uniquely a poet; I have taken several routes. Poems, plays, narratives (short story and novel) have been less options than necessities regarding this matter of writing (*matter: *as soon as I write this word I reveal my belief in the act of writing* about something; *I write about a world distant from writing).*

In poems I sustain the most fragile and the most perishable, the emotion of the instant, the unreproducible, the feeling that the horizon embraces everything but, because it isn't pertinent or because it is implicit, it disappears without a visible trace: if I write poems it is to hold onto that which is condemned to evaporate. If I've already said that I write about what remains outside of writing (phenomenon, the mystery of art), in the poems I try to write about what can't be discussed from the world that is hidden outside of words and that conforms to us without naming us: darkness, love, uncertainty, our own unknown selves, better even: not one of these words but the world that gives breath to our inert bodies of mud . . .

AGUA OSCURA

Es hablar de la llanura que se quiebra en la noche,
interminablemente oscura,
que se desborda al horizonte, silenciosa y sin límite

El círculo roto, el murmullo que desatendido
  se multiplica,
se convierte en un ejército con mil frentes,
sonido inacabable,
incomprensión inacabable

  (es tu olor la firmeza única,
  la única sobrevivencia del sabor del día)

Tengo abiertas las manos para tocar la caída
  de agua oscura que en múltiples texturas se desenmaraña
He abierto conscientemente las manos: nada
  me detiene, nada detengo. En esta limpia
  fluidez tumultuosa perdí el modo de jugar la ronda:
En este movimiento he dejado el último resquicio virgen
  al movimiento, el último e infinito resguardo.

Ya nada me distingue del mundo.

   ◆

DARK WATER

The plain that breaks all night,
the silent horizon brimming
with darkness

The broken circle,
the whisper that multiplies, neglected,
into an army with a thousand fronts—
unending sound,
unending incomprehension

> (Your scent is the only bearing left,
> the only aftertaste of the day.)

My hands are open to the dark waterfall
        unraveling its textures
I have consciously opened my hands: nothing holds me
        back, I hold back nothing. It was in this clear
        turbulence I stopped playing hide-and-seek.
In this movement I have given the last unsealed opening
        to movement, the final guardian.

There is nothing to tell me apart from the world.

◆

—Sí tú eres la firmeza única,
el momento cierto que espera a un lado de
la noche para abordarme,
pero eres el único eco capaz de nombrar lo
        que ejerce la oscuridad sobre la llanura—

Ya nada me distingue del mundo porque nada detengo. Pero (sopla lento el viento) cada partícula de polvo, cada gota de agua que viene en el viento, un instante antes de entrar en mí se detiene. Nada me distingue del mundo, es cierto, pero nada me traspasa. Todo, justo un instante antes de perforarme, me señala, me sostiene, me demarca.

—Yes, you are my only bearing,
the exact moment waiting at one side
of the night to board me.
But you are also the only echo that can say
what force it is that night
exerts on the plain—

There is nothing to tell me apart from the world because I hold back
nothing. But (the wind is blowing slowly) each particle of dust, each
raindrop brought by the wind, just before coming into me, holds itself
back. Nothing can tell me apart from the world, but nothing passes
through me. Everything, an instant before piercing me, sustains me,
signals me, defines my shape.

Translated by Brady Earnhart

LA FIGURA

Es la sola figura todo el intrincado lapso,
el laberinto trazado laberinto hasta el exceso

◆

La precisa sombra de los brazos
se olvida de sí al tocar los muslos,
se moldea a los muslos,
acaba haciéndose carne en los muslos:

El párpado, la pierna, el dedo:
desordenada la figura en sí se pierde
y nada, ni ella misma, la alcanza,
ni aún aquella que, tumbada sobre su propio
        cuerpo, cabalga . . .

◆

el intrincado lapso,
el brinco que se sostiene en el espacio,
el sordo salto que no toca la tierra
                —pero es un salto, es
                un brinco, no es nada
                sino tierra, sino
                ausencia de tierra—
el hueco impulso sobre el polvo,

THE FIGURE

The whole intricate lapse, labyrinth
upon labyrinth ad nauseam, a lone figure.

◆

The arm's precise shadow
loses track of itself
as it touches the thighs,
finally becoming flesh of the thighs:

The eyelid, the leg, the finger:
everything out of place, the figure loses her way
in herself, and no one can reach her,
not even she herself,
not even she that, lying down
        on her own body, rides . . .

◆

the intricate lapse,
the deaf leap held in space
        —but it is a leap;
        it is nothing
        but ground, but
        absence of ground—
the hollow impulse over the dust

el que en medio de sí mismo se subleva y se
      desangra.

Laberinto hasta el exceso.
La menor división de nuevo se fragmenta,
y la figura
(la fría idea de que todo el cuerpo es una sola carne)
sin dejar de estar ahí—todos la vemos—se
      pierde . . .

rearing in the core of itself, to bleed.

♦

Labyrinth *ad nauseum.*
The smallest division splits itself again,
and the figure
(the cold idea that the body is all one flesh)
still there where we can see her
loses her way . . .

Translated by Brady Earnhart

DE LUZ Y SOMBRA

(Aunque aquello que llega aleteando,
agitándose en la altura para alcanzar su vuelo
sea mi nombre . . .)

No puedo permanecer oscura frente a esto.
   Se deshace una olorosa trenza sobre el día,
sobre la mañana que admirable se puebla de
olores vivos, de juegos esparcidos donde la
sombra toca lo que hace un instante era luz y
donde la luz toca lo que era sombra, formando
un enrejado infinito

   Una aguja de luz y sombra entra y sale en
los segundos, los atraviesa vigorosa:
   no los distorsiona:
   los despierta a sí mismos

   Y tu piel
me obliga sin muecas ni sonrisas, no a darme,
a apoderarme de mí

   Más sola que nunca
porque en el mar sin olas, en la tela tensada
hasta nunca acabarse, no hay nadie que me escuche
y, es cierto, he perdido el punto de retorno

LIGHT AND SHADOW

(Even if the thing that arrives,
its fin above me trembling toward flight,
is my own name . . .)

How can I stay dark here.
A fragrant braid relaxes over the day,
over the morning populated with colors, with games
that scatter when a shadow touches what was,
an instant ago, light,
and light touches what was shadow—
an infinite latticework.

A needle of shadow goes in and out
of the seconds, flickers across them;
they are not distorted but brought to themselves

Articulating nothing
your skin compels me not to surrender

but to take hold of myself.

Lonelier than ever
because in a sea without waves, in cloth
so taut it never ends, there is no one to listen
to me, and I know I can never go back

Mientras todos permanecen con las piernas

cruzadas y fumando, seguros como ante un
espejo, yo no puedo dejar de oír la voz que sin
guiarme me despierta, que sin decir hacia dónde
dirigirme me arrebata la patria

   —siento cómo me crece, cercano a la
cara, el pelo, despacio, minucioso, como luchando
contra la forma en que intenta fijarlo inmóvil la luz
   y siento cómo de los poros se desliza, no tan silencioso
como debiera, el sudor, devastando el vapor estéril
de la virginidad, de la inmovilidad y la resistencia.

   Después, ya de regreso, viendo todo en el
desorden, una voz estrecha como un pasillo sin
fondo, intenta levantar un inventario para
regresarme a la lenta, fluida corriente de aire
que de flanco a flanco de la tarde permanece serena

     de flanco a flanco de la tarde

   Pero si yo soy, o fui hace un instante, las
ancas tensas y extensas franqueando los
innombrables puentes levadizos, franqueando el
tumultuoso viento, la arena volátil, equinas y
brillantes y sin relajar un instante su pureza

En ti la irrupción que me levanta,
que vertical me subleva, me desordena, me
    obliga

Que me desconoce y, saciada en sí misma, me
    retorna;
me acerca más al punto de donde provengo,
    de lo que antes, cercana a mí misma, estuve.

While everyone sits smoking, with their legs

crossed, as confident as they would be in front of
mirrors, I keep hearing a voice—it wakes me up
without guiding me; without telling me where we
are going makes me leave home

    —I can feel myself growing, around my
face, my hair, slowly, minutely, as if fighting
against the shape the light tries to hold
    and I can feel my sweat coming, not as quietly
as it should, to my pores, ruining the sterile
odor of virginity, of immobility and resistance.

Afterwards, already on its way back, seeing
everything in disorder, a voice like an endless
hallway tries to tell me why I should return
to the slow air which, from flank to flank
of the afternoon, remains serene

        from flank to flank of the afternoon

but if I am, or was an instant ago, the tense,
splayed haunches that opened bridges without
names, opened the tumultuous air, the volatile
sand, equine and brilliant and not relaxing
for an instant their purity

In you, the invasion that moves me to rebel,
puts me on my feet, makes
a mess of me, obligates me

That ignores me and, satiated with itself,
sends me back, sends me

nearer to where I was when I was near myself.

Vertical me hieres para revelarme las distancias
        disparadas que se aproximan.

                        ◆

Entonces
mi piel no excede en nada de la noche. Nada
        la mira.
No sopla el viento y los árboles recargan sus
        hojas sobre sí mismos
(otra noche, hasta los retoños se sostenían en
        su sombra, sobre el piso. Y pisar las sombras
        era esparcir un olor a hierba).

Es la sombra del árbol dibujo minucioso
        trazado por la blanca mano de la Luna.

On my feet you wound me, to show me the disparate
horizons closing.

♦

So there is nothing my skin does
that night is not better at. Nothing
is watching.
The wind does not blow; the trees pile leaves on themselves
(another night, even the shoots were held in its
shadow. And to step on the shadows was to
disseminate an odor of grass).

The tree's shadow is an immaculate drawing
traced by the white hand of the Moon.

Translated by Brady Earnhart

Kyra Galván

Before Kyra Galván (born in 1956) studied for her master's degree in economics at the School of Economics from 1976 through 1980, she studied poetry with Juan Banuelos at the National Autonomous University of Mexico. She received a scholarship to study with Hernan Lavin Cerda, and in 1980 she was awarded first place in the Francisco Gonzalez de Leon competition for young poets. In 1982-83, Galván was awarded a fellowship from El Centro Mexicano de Escritores in Mexico City, where, for the most part, she worked on the book *Alabanza Escribo*. She has given readings throughout Mexico and the provinces.

Galván's publications include: *Un pequeno moreton en la piel de nadie* (1980), *Un tren de luz* (1982), and translations of Anna Akhmatova and Dylan Thomas. Her most recent book of poems, from Coleccion Molinos de Viento, is *Alabanza Escribo* (1989). Kyra Galván lives in Mexico City, but in 1987 and 1988 she lived in Japan from where she wrote the following note.

◆

The bio-bibliography is easy enough to write, but at this moment it is difficult for me to clearly formulate an idea of where I am going as a woman or as a poet, *because I am not entirely sure. I am living through a period of great change, as you might imagine, here in a country that demands that the stranger takes pains to adapt. It is a fascinating place, but I am having trouble adjusting.*

I am writing an essay about the historical problem of the social differences between men and women, and I hope, later, to write something about Japan. And of course I want to finish a new book of poems.

PORQUE LA VIDA CORRE Y NO SUCEDE

La vida corre y se sucede por todas partes
por todos los caminos lejanos a la urbe.
Hay un constante movimiento en las carreteras:
pipas gusano en las crestas de la montaña
camiones de carga y de pasajeros.
Los campos de trigo y los maizales
        no se detienen nunca
corren a la misma velocidad
que las torres eléctricas.
Y ahí están con sus sombreros,
vendiendo naranjas y aguacates,
embriagándose con pulque,
paseándose con sus chaquetas burdas
viendo pasar a las hembritas.
El silencio recorre su piel a golpes lentos
maleándola, abollándola,
abriéndola en ausencia pastosa.
La vida vibra y resplandece
llena de cáscaras de fruta y escupitajos.
Vienen los capitales a remodelar sus plazas
y a llenar las calles de faroles,
pero no penetran la piel curtida
estirada con agua salada de soledades.
Y las mujeres se hincan.
Y rezan los rosarios y los padrenuestros.
Y el cristo ensangrentado devuelve la mirada,

WHY LIFE RUNS ON AND DOES NOT HAPPEN

Life runs on and occurs everywhere
on all the distant roads to the city
There is a continuous motion on the highway
worm tanks on top of the mountain
trucks with freight and passengers
The wheat fields and the corn fields
        never take a rest
they run at the same speed
as the high tension towers
And there they are with their hats
selling oranges and avocados
getting sloshed on pulque
out cruising in their sleazy jackets
watching the chicks go by
The silence goes over its skin with slow blows
bruising it denting it
opening it into doughy absence
Life trembles and shines
full of fruit rind and spit
The capitals come to remodel their squares
and fill their streets with lampposts
but they never get through the tanned skin
stretched tight with the salt water of loneliness
And the women kneel down
And they say their beads and their prayers
And the blood-stained Christ returns their stare

pero no la palabra.
¿O tal vez, sí, devuelva el aliento?
De todos modos, las manos les arden humeantes
pelando chiles y cardando lana.
Los huicholes y los coras
descubren su animal protector
con un "trago" de peyote.
Sorprendidos por el futuro
se deslizan entre dos dimensiones
con sus cuerpos de camino forzado,
con su aliento abierto a puñetazos,
con la brecha que dejan
las palabras omitidas
        en el juego erótico.

          but not a word
or maybe, yes, did he breathe?
Anyway the hot hands smolder
peeling chilies and carding wool
The *huicholes* and the *coras*
discover their animal guardian
with a hit of peyote
Surprised by the future
they slide between two dimensions
with their bodies beaten down like roads
with their breath punched open
with the hole left
by the words never said
in bed

                              Translated by W. S. Merwin

URBANA

El campo es para mí
una realidad lejana.
Ni siquiera puedo mentir su distancia
cuando se aleja el amor.
No pretendo enternecerme cerca de un sembradío
porque mis manos no sienten la tierra.
Sólo conozco colmenas de acero.
Aquí te hundes en la violencia instantánea
y no tienes miedo
de que te den o quiten la tierra.
Aquí estás despojado,
perteneces a la nada de nadie.
No crees ni en la lluvia prefabricada
cayendo de quién sabe cuál inventos modernos.
Corremos de un edificio a otro y el cielo
se niega constante. También el amor niega.
Y en un abrir y cerrar de ojos
aprendes y desaprendes los ritos asfálticos.
Te vuelves explorador de islas multitudinarias,
experto conductor de conversaciones truncas.

No tienes tierra.
Deberías arrullar el concreto, pero,

CITY WOMAN

For me the country
is a distant reality.
I can't even disguise its distance
when love goes away.
I don't pretend to go all soft at the sight of a plowed field
because my hands don't feel the earth.
The only beehives I know are made of steel.
Here you sink in the violence of an instant
and don't worry
about them giving or taking away from your land.
Here you are dispossessed
and belong to the nothing of nobody.
You don't believe in the prefabricated rain
falling from who knows what modern inventions.
We run from one building to another and the sky
says no the whole time. Loves says no too.
And in the blink of an eye
you learn and unlearn the rites of asphalt.
You return to explore the innumerable islands,
expert conductor of cutoff conversations.

You have no land.
You ought to court the concrete, but

no tienes ligas con nada, ¿cómo tenerlas?

No. El campo y el amor nunca empiezan.
Y tú sabes
que los mitos urbanos no se interrumpen.

you have no connections with anything—how could you?

No. The country and love never begin.
And you know
that the myths of the city continue without a break.

Translated by W. S. Merwin

BELLAS ARTES

Mientras dormías escuchaba tu resuello,
profundo y lento.
Diríase que hasta joven.
Quién podría decir
que bajo tu corazón pesaban
tantos años de ser la maestra
en el arte de la sumisión
en la virtud de la mudez
en el vicio de no tocar.

BELLAS ARTES

While you slept I heard you breathing,
deep and slow.
One would say it sounded young.
Who could tell
that under your heart weighed
so many years of being the expert
in the art of submission
in the virtue of muteness
in the vice of not touching.

Translated by Zoe Anglesey

ESCOMBROS DE CANTO

I.

Sobre el cosmos escribo esta historia
y busco el comienzo del poema
        en el pozo olvidado de mi ciudad.
Busco la bahía de concreto,
la vista sobrevuela los muros
y vierto lágrimas
sobre el atardecer naranja
y el semáforo sordo.

II.

En lo alto de mi cabeza
se ha instalado un pajarillo que no canta.
Entre dos dedos sostengo mis labios
mientras un ligero dolor acecha:
me convenzo de que estoy en el infierno.
Los ojos se dilatan ante la realidad
pero, ¿para qué llorar?
El abrazo no fue suficientemente demoledor.
Entre nuestros cuerpos desnudos se coló la soledad.
        Siempre había prisa.
        Para alcanzar otra orilla.
        Llegar al sitio que es el *No lugar*.

DEBRIS OF SONG

I.

This story is about the cosmos
and as I write I look for the poem's beginning
        in the forgotten spring of my city.
In pursuit of the concrete bay
my gaze flies out over the walls
my tears rain down on
the orange afternoon
and the hush of traffic lights.

II.

A little bird who doesn't sing
has taken up residence on top of my head.
I purse my lips between two fingers
while a slight pain lurks:
I persuade myself this is Hell.
Facing reality, my eyes fill with tears
but what is the use of crying?
Our embrace wasn't crushing enough.
Loneliness slipped between our naked bodies.
        We were always in a hurry.
        To get to the other side.
        To get to that *Nowhere* place.

¿Por qué animales seremos tan humanos?
¿Por qué de nuestras piernas
        sólo escapa la nostalgia
        y de nuestras voces-teléfono
sólo recogemos escombros de canto,
cosquillas en la punta de los dedos?

III.

Créeme / créeme
que alguna vez esperé
sábanas limpias en cama matrimonial
        t.v. a las 10 p.m.
cine los viernes y reunión familiar los domingos.
Créeme, alguna vez pensé
que la ciudad no era laberinto
que llegaría a ser estúpidamente feliz
y sin perderme una sola / pasaría
las cenas de nochebuena
en la misma postura / con idéntica sonrisa
        deslumbrada por el flash.
Que la soledad sería algo pasajero,
una pequeña molestia, acné de adolescencia.
Pero nunca creí que buscaría tu olor
en las construcciones de cemento,
una pista en los alambres de luz.
Ay, ciudad, ¿por qué te tragas a ti misma?

IV.

Me duele el mundo de los hombres.
Con sus picos y palas
han levantado este escenario.
Nosotras somos intrusas

What animals made us so human?
Why does only longing
        escape from our legs
        why do we cull only
        the debris of song
        from our telephone voices,
        a prickling at our fingertips?

III.

Believe me / Believe me
once I hoped for
clean sheets on a marriage bed
        TV at ten
Friday movies and family on Sundays.
Believe me, I once thought
that the city was no labyrinth
that I could be stupidly happy
that without missing a single one / I'd
spend Christmas dinners
in the same position / with the same dazzle
of a flashbulb smile.
That loneliness would be a passing,
minor complaint, adolescent acne.
I never thought I'd be tracking your smell
through cement buildings
a trail of electrical wires.
Oh, City, why do you swallow yourself?

IV.

The world of men pains me.
They have dug up this scene
with shovels and picks.

acostumbradas a vivir entre sangre
y sentir humedad caliente entre las piernas.
Amansamos nuestros miedos
y sentimos coraje por la vergüenza al sexo
y a la vida, que nos inculcaron nuestras madres.
Hemos comenzado a amar nuestros cuerpos.
Por eso me resisto / a venderme /
a dejarme vencer de cualquier otra forma.
Ser fuerte a pesar de las angustias.
Rodeada de estrellas / infinito / y rayos solares
que se nutren de mis heridas,
estoy cercada por un tiempo que no es el mío.
Doblo barrotes de soledad y displacer
        dentro de sueños alargados donde
la razón se expande más allá de los razonamientos.

V.

Ya no puedes volver.
Hay que cerrar los ojos / apretar las mandíbulas
los puños / el diafragma / aguantar la respiración
y sólo entonces atreverse a mover las piernas
abrir los ojos / la boca:
gritar.
Atravesar los días con preguntas nuevecitas.
Amar las respuestas que nos horadaron la piel.

We women are intruders
familiar with blood
and damp heat between our legs.
We tame our fears
and feel rage at the shame
for sex and life
our mothers instilled in us.
We have started to love our bodies.
That's why I refuse to sell out
or be repressed in any other way.
To be strong in spite of the pain.
Surrounded by stars / infinity / sunbeams
that feed on my wounds I am
walled in by a time that isn't mine.
I bend back the bars of loneliness and vexation
in lengthy dreams where reason
stretches further than reasons.

V.

You can't come back anymore.
You have to close your eyes / clench your teeth
fists / diaphragm / hold your breath
and only then dare to move your legs
open your eyes / mouth:
scream.
Go through the days with brand-new questions.
Love the answers that pierced our skin.

Translated by Janet Rodney

CONVERSACIÓN CON EMILY DICKINSON

El primer impulso fue llamarte por teléfono. Correr y marcar tu número, pero ¿cuál es tu número? Larga distancia es el tiempo. Quisiera presentarme: Miss Dickinson I introduce you . . . pero no sabría qué decir. Tal vez preguntarte por Carlo, tu perro, única compañía masculina, además de tu padre por supuesto.

> *Dime si mi verso está vivo.*

Vivos, que nuestros versos estuvieran *vivos* es lo que nosotros quisiéramos. Vivos como la Historia, como la vida que nos corre por el cuerpo y lo que nos rodea y matamos. Porque estoy rodeada de oscuridad. De objetos y más objetos. Unos libros, un radio, una máquina, una cama que es usada por mí, y yo, que soy usada por este silencio que me roba vida. El radio no parlotea y el mundo no sabe de mí. Estoy aquí encerrada como lo estuviste tú en los verdes campos de Massachussetts.

Quiero que sea esta línea la más dura autocrítica.

> *Me gustaría aprender. ¿Podrías decirme cómo crecer o es algo natural, como la melodía o el hechizo?*

Natural como un plié con las piernas hacia afuera. Como quien escribe una carta al mundo que nunca le escribe. Como quien no sabe ser mujer hasta que es demasiado tarde. Como quien vive con unas cuantas líneas de poesía al día, con unos cuantos roces, unos cuantos acordes, unos cuantos movimientos. Me he bastado con gentes que nunca acaricio, con silencios extensísimos entre los extraños, ésos que nunca pisan nuestra casa.

CONVERSATION WITH EMILY DICKINSON

My first impulse was to call you. Rush and dial your number, but what is your number? Long distance is time. I'd like to meet you: Miss Dickinson, may I introduce . . . but I wouldn't know what to say. Maybe I'd ask you about your dog Carlo, your only male company, except for your father of course.

Tell me if my poetry is alive

Alive, that's what we want, our poetry to be *alive*. Alive like history, like life coursing through our bodies, like everything around us that we kill. Because I am surrounded by darkness. By things and more things. A few books, a radio, a typewriter, a bed I have use of, and I who am used by this silence stealing my life. The radio is quiet and I am unknown to the world. I'm as trapped here as you were in the green fields of Massachusetts.

I want this line to be the hardest on myself.

I want to learn. Could you tell me how I can grow or is that something that comes naturally, like melody or witchcraft?

As naturally as a deep plié. Or someone writing a letter to the world who never writes it. Or a woman who doesn't know how to be one until it's too late. Or someone who gets along on a few lines of poetry every day, on a few caresses, a few chords, a few movements. I've made do with people I never caress, with endless silences among strangers, the ones that

Pero la muerte fue demasiado para mí en aquel entonces.

Fue más de lo que yo podía manejar y me dejó esparcida, atomizada. De pronto me perdí, como quien pierde un poema una tarde de lluvia. Todos los escalofríos eran inútiles, todo intento de lucha, estéril. Permanecí durante mucho tiempo midiendo mis respiraciones. ¿Por qué tanto terror a equivocarse?

Hay un bamboleo continuo en las orillas de las afirmaciones. ¿No crees? Antagonismos de dos existencias.

Lo más duro es aprender a cuidarse, así, sin aspavientos.

Tal vez te rías de mí. No voy a detenerme por eso.

Ahora me encuentro en la Sixtina
porque soy una sibila de Miguel Ángel
con las piernas desnudas, listas a pasar a la inmortalidad.
Desnudez de espacios para los que no sabemos mirar.
Para que busquemos el otro mundo. Para que se anulen las fuerzas
gravitatorias y el cosmos se me vuelva neutral y entre a mi
organismo complementario:
                    al tú, al tí, al té.

El espejo se me gastó de tanto mirarme en él, pero no así la cara, que ahora resplandece y logra encenderse hasta cobrar una intensidad translúcida.

Me veo: soy un espectro.

Necesitaré una marquesina para anunciar mi revelación.

Mi incumbencia es el círculo.

never set foot in our house.

But death was too much for me way back then.

It was more than I could handle and it left me scattered and broken. I lost
myself suddenly, like you might lose a poem on a rainy afternoon. Shud-
dering was useless, struggle hopeless. I watched my breath for a long time.
Why so terrified of being wrong?

At the edge of affirmation there's a continuous wavering, don't you think?
Two realities quarreling.

Looking out for oneself like that, without hassle, is what's hardest.

Maybe you think this is funny. That won't stop me.

Right now I'm in the Sistine Chapel
because I'm one of Michelangelo's sibyls,
legs bared for immortality.
Bare spaces for those who don't know how to look.
So we can look for the other world. So gravity
can be banished and the cosmos neutralized
and enter my being next
                    to ye, to you, to your.

I wore out my mirror from so much looking but now my face glows and
kindles to the point of translucence.

I see myself: I am a ghost.

I'm going to need a billboard to announce my revelation.

My incumbency is the circle.

El mundo se ve en tus ojos de mil maneras distintas, porque todos (y cada uno) tienen su manera de negar el mundo; la realidad, Emily. Nos deslizamos en círculos de apariencia recta. Parto de mis senos maternales para llegar a mis senos cicatrizados, un poco más adolorida que siempre, creyendo que el mundo está vacío, pero se trata solamente de una especie de incapacidad vital, es el intento de penetrar en el otro mundo que no es el nuestro, es el intento de amar, el estar intentando siempre, como si vivir fuera tan fácil, es el inventarnos a través de otra persona que no ha existido nunca, es el creer que crecemos y somos adultos. Y que somos capaces de amar, que el espejo somos nosotros y que podemos casarnos y tener hijos y ser abuelas algún día.

¿Y dónde quedas tú, Emilia?

Es el estar creyendo siempre en el libre albedrío, pero la Historia es más cruel de lo que nosotros pensamos.

Porque la Historia, un día, nos mata.

Through your eyes I can see the world in a thousand different ways because they all (each in its way) have a way of negating the world; reality, Emily. We slide around in circles that seem straight. I leave my mother's breasts to get my own scarred ones, a little more painfully than usual, believing the world is empty, but it's only a kind of not being able, an attempt to penetrate the other world that isn't ours, an attempt to love, always an attempt. As if living were that easy, projecting through another person who never existed, believing we grow and are grown up. That we can love, that we are the mirror and will someday marry, have children and be grandmothers.

And where does that leave you, Emily?

Keeping faith in free will. But History is crueler than we think.

Because History one day kills us.

Translated by Janet Rodney

Elena Milán

I was born in the village of Real del Catorce, in San Luis Potosi, Mexico.
I am a translator and interpreter, with a diploma from the Institute of
Translation and Interpretation in Mexico City. But presently, I am
employed as a technical translator by the Federal Commission of Electricity,
the electrical industry owned and run by the government.

In large part, I owe my literary formation to the two years I studied in
the United States, the two years I studied French language and literature in
Paris, and the free workshops at the Autonomous State University of
Mexico where I was a student of Juan Banuelos, Tito Monterroso, Miguel
Donoso Pareja, as well as of the master Iverna Codina.

I have published two books of poems, *Circuito Amores y Anexas* with the
Latitudes Press and *Corredor Secreto* with Antares Press. At present I am
preparing a book of short stories tentatively titled *Ocho Pecados Conventuales.*

◆

*Fundamentally I have followed in the footsteps of Saint Teresa insofar as she
claimed to have written as she spoke. Aside from her, I have been attracted to the
classical poetry of Quevedo, Lope de Vega, and Zorilla, and to more modern poets like
Lorca, Salinas, Alexandre, Machado, Parra, and Sabines. I should emphasize as well
my debt to Efrain Huerta and Rosario Castellanos. Nor can I forget to mention some
of the English writers such as Elizabeth Barrett Browning and Edna Saint Vincent
Millay.*

*Those who have placed me within the anti-poetic tradition have been accurate, for
I tend to develop my themes with both irony and a simple, direct sarcasm. At times
the poem is almost journalistic, a loud bell to awaken consciousness. I believe in what
Marco Antonio Campos says about poetry not following the mainstream of the
country.*

*Of late, I have tended toward the short story, and I have also begun to experiment
with play writing.*

FOLKLORE

Y a pesar de nuestras caras sonrientes,
          nuestra música saltimbanqui,
          nuestros sombreros para retar al viento
seguimos siendo los perdedores:
sus cañones contra nuestros banderines de papel de china,
          contra nuestro amor al sol y la altura;
sus armas frente a nuestras bolas de nieve y los fuegos de artificio.
Sin embargo, continuamos bailando por las calles
al ritmo de las sonajas y las flautas de mil carrizos,
entre el resquebrajarse de las olas y su tronar multicolor,
entre las alas del ángel y el diablo barba de chivo.
Pero recuerda, hace siglos, en Siam
la danza era el adiestramiento diario.

FOLKLORE

And in spite of our beaming faces
            our charlatan music,
            our hats for defying the wind
we continue to be the lost ones:
their cannons against our paper and porcelain flags,
            against our love of sun and heights;
their weapons facing our snowballs and fireworks.
Nevertheless, we go dancing through the streets
to the rhythm of rattles and clarinets with a thousand reeds,
between the toppling waves and their multicolored thunder,
between the wings of the angel and the goateed fiend.
But remember, centuries ago, in Siam
the dance was daily training.

Translated by Forrest Gander

ALUCINACIÓN I

Supongamos que una zona del mundo se ha unido
del Atlántico al Pacífico,
de Portugal al Japón;
desde el Mediterráneo y Mar del Norte,
al Artico hacia el este.
Supongamos que soplan mitos extraños
desde la viejas cavernas de Altamira
y la ruinas del Turkistán,
algo así como naves vikingas
y nuevas leyendas de tártaros y samurais.
Supongamos que el gobierno yanki no les gusta
y deciden desestabilizarlo.

HALLUCINATION I

Let's suppose a zone of the world falls together
from Atlantic to Pacific,
from Portugal to Japan;
from the Mediterranean to the North Sea
to the eastern Arctic.
Let's suppose strange myths lift
from the ancient caves of Altamira
and the ruins of Turkistan,
something like Viking ships
and fresh legends of Tartars and samurai
Let's suppose the Yankee government doesn't please them
and they decide to destabilize it.

Translated by Forrest Gander

CORAZON DE DINOSAURIA

Es inútil

jamás comprenderías a este corazón de dinosaurio

—Jorge Boccanera

Siglos de civilización dan a tu espalda
la interrogante forma de una clave de fa,
qué peso de dunas, prejuicios, historias,
para tu clave sin sonido:
la estrella fugaz ya no acuatiza en tus ojos.
Déjame ayudarte con el fardo, soy fuerte:
hace varias eras me dividí en dos
y la vida de otro me iluminó el camino.
Yo llevo el peso del fuego y el agua
y soy igualmente primitiva.
Déjame compartir mi carga,
decirte que te amo desde hace millones de años.

DINOSAUR HEART

It is useless

sufficient you could comprehend this dinosaur heart

                                        —*Jorge Boccanera*

Centuries of civilization fall upon your back
the interrogative form in the key of F,
duress of shifting sands, prejudices, stories,
for your soundless note:
the shooting star no longer alights in your eyes.
Let me help you with your burden, I am strong:
Some time ago I divided into two
and the life of the other lit up my path.
I carried the weight of water and fire
and am equally primitive.
Let me share my load,
to tell you I've loved you for a million years.

                                        Translated by Zoe Anglesey

▼▼

ACOSO

Voz iluminada como un cuaderno,
viva voz sutil, ironía de lija,
perseguidora, sin trastienda, nueva.
Voz aurora para armar un relato,
enloquecer de mujeres en marcha.
Voz cabello rubio, tan daga, lirio,
alfiletero, porcelana, almendra.
Voz plantada en la palma de mi mano
con todo un cuerpo de estrofas, leyendas
y la música más renacimiento.
Voz para la más bragada entereza.
¿En dónde están los que no te tienen, voz,
que el oído no se presta a contestarte?
Déjame, te ordeno, no me persigas,
no resuenes más como la esperanza,
que arañas la piel. Que rehúso oírte:
me sacas infinitas ganas de pelea,
todo lo que me queda de insurgente.
Basta. Que me niego a escuchar, he dicho.
Calla, por lo más santo en Guatemala.
Calla: no quiero imaginar siquiera,
desaparecida, lo que te han hecho,

RELENTLESS PURSUIT

Voice illuminated like a notebook,
subtle vibrant voice, grating irony,
indicting, courageous, new,
an early dawn voice to begin a story,
to stir women on the march.
Blond hair voice, so dagger, lily,
pin cushion, porcelain, almond-like.
Voice planted in the palm of my hand
with a whole body of verse, legends
and nothing less than renaissance music.
Voice for the most virgin of thighs.
And where are they, voice, who
do not lend an ear to answer you?
Allow me, I command you, don't persecute me,
nothing resounds more than hope's
goose bumps on skin. I refuse to hear you:
you provoke my infinite desire to struggle
and all that remains insurgent in me.
Okay! I've said I catch myself listening.
Quiet, for the most saintly in Guatemala.
Quiet: I can't even imagine—
what they have done to you,

a vos,
     Alaíde Foppa,
               mi amiga.

a disappeared,
   Alaide Foppa,*
     my friend.

           Translated by Zoe Anglesey

*Alaide Foppa entered Mexico as an exile, along with her husband, who was a minister in the elected Jacobo Arbenz government of Guatemala and who was overthrown in a U.S.- and C.I.A.-sponsored coup in 1954. She founded the first feminist magazine of Latin America, *FEM*. Early in the 1980s she returned to Guatemala to visit her mother, who was very elderly and ill. She was captured and disappeared.

VIAJE AL SUR

Pero qué hacer entre este puente y el próximo,
cómo jalar al río de los cabellos, mostrarle la fetidez del cauce:
que no es por allí ni por acá:
el lecho debe ser escarbado nuevamente.
Los profetas dejaron de tener razón,
los brujos se extinguieron y los redentores han sido ametrallados.
Sólo quedan uñas y dientes, puños y pies:
la desnudez que endurece las entrañas,
esa mirada que lengüetea un sabor a sangre y comienza a correr.

TRIP SOUTH

But what to do between this bridge and the next,
how to pull the river up by its hair, to show its fetid bottom:
which is neither here nor there:
the riverbed should be redug.
The prophets stopped being right,
the shamans became extinct and the redeemers have been gunned down.
Only nails and teeth remain, fists and feet:
that nakedness which toughens the gut,
that look which licks and savors blood, and begins to run.

Translated by Zoe Anglesey

FRENTE A FRENTE

Como puta vieja añoras tu juventud y repites anécdotas, pero sabes que nadie cree en tí, ni tú misma. Sigues siendo codiciosa y despiadada: aún representas peligro: todavía son buenos tu puntería y tu caballo y puedes pagarte todo, incluso gigolós. En la cima de tu historia fuiste generosa tras ser bien pagada, y bastante hábil para salvar las apariencias, tanto, que mi padre creía en tí, que eras el camino seguro. Cuando renegaste de tu principio se supo engañado y sin salida, y se volvió silencioso. Cuando yo te escupí la cara, tuvo miedo. Permitió el exabrupto, jamás la acción. Me hice clandestina; algo se había agrietado para siempre. Ya no te llamabas esperanza, ni futuro. El alcanzó a oler tu descomposición. Estuvo en tu subasta: a cuánto el camión de arena movediza, y hubo otra quebradura. Ahora ya no hacen falta permisos. Sus hijos te miramos de frente. Conocemos tus más recientes zarpazos, penosos esfuerzos para ponerte de pie, avanzar de nuevo. Y sus hijos, los que nunca fueron tuyos, te preguntamos cómo va tu oficio, buscona, y no te perdonamos.

FACE TO FACE

Like an old whore you miss your youth so you repeat the same anecdotes knowing no one believes you, you don't believe yourself. Still greedy and ruthless: still a threat: still riding high in the saddle with your dead eye, paying your way, hiring gigolos. When you made it to the top you were generous with all that money you were paid, and fairly clever at saving face, so my father believed in you, took you for the real thing. When you reneged on your principles, he knew he'd been taken, no way out, and he closed up. When I spit in your face, that scared him. He permitted back talk, but never action. I had to go underground; something broke forever. You had already stopped talking of chances, of a future. He got a whiff of your rot. He was on your auction block: how much for a truckload of quicksand, and then came another rupture. Now your excuses don't fly. His kids, we look you between the eyes. We've heard about the recent reverses, the painful efforts to get you to your feet, pointed straight ahead. And his children, who were never yours, we ask after your affairs, you slut, and we forgive you nothing.

Translated by Forrest Gander

CRUCIGRAMA I

Ambiciosa, demasiado bronca
para ser florecita de durazno,
tanto, que a pesar de tu dulce color
no te importa andar en tratos
con la internacional fascista del Cono Sur.
Ah, si aparecieras
en diarios italianos y sureños
extrayendo del sombrero de copa
respuestas a las más célebres intrigas,
podrías, con nuevos oropeles,
aspirar a la mano del príncipe heredero.

WORD PUZZLE I

Ambitious, too brazen
to be a little peach blossom,
so much so that in spite of your luscious color
it doesn't bother you—making deals
with the fascist internationale of the Southern Cone.*
Ah, if you'd appeared
in Italian papers and southerly winds
pulling out of the hat
answers to the most celebrated intrigues
you might, with new graciousness,
seek the hand of the heir to the throne.

Translated by Zoe Anglesey

*The Southern Cone refers to Chile, Argentina, and Uruguay.

Gloria Gervitz

Born in Mexico City on March 29, 1943, Gloria Gervitz studied art history at the Iberoamerican University. Her poetry has been included in several anthologies. *Shajarit*, her first book, was published in 1979, and it was followed by *Fragmento de Ventana* (1986) and *Yiskor* (1987). Her translations of Anna Akhmatova, Marguerite Yourcenar, Samuel Beckett, Clarice Lispector, Nadezdha Mandelstam, and Rita Dove have been published in magazines. *Migraciones* (1991), a new book of her collected works, was published by El Fondo de Cultura Economica. In 1992, she received a fellowship for one year from the Consejo Nacional para las Artes y la Cultura.

◆

It takes me years to write a poem; it grows slowly inside me like a tree. In writing, there is always something that remains obscure, wrapped in mystery. Anyway, it is the poem that chooses us. In my poetry there are voices of my Jewish women ancestors who arrived in Mexico before the Second World War as exiles from Russia; their voices merge with the more ancient voice of my Mexican grandmother, who was a Roman Catholic. But memory betrays us, for it is associated with forgetfulness and death; it is like a fishing net with holes. Perhaps it is because of this that my work attempts a small homage to these women who never had the time to speak of their dreams. They had to work hard in order to put bread on the table, to keep clothes washed, to send children to school. And nevertheless, their dreams brought them to Mexico and their dreams sustained them for the whole of their lives. In Fragmento de Ventana, *the first part of my long poem* Migraciones, *I wrote that someone should weep for these women, and I believe it is me who weeps for them so that their own tears aren't lost. The second part,* Del Libra de Yiskor, *is an invocation, a dialogue between someone who has been exiled and the poet who poses questions. Only a few words are ever lifted from oblivion and brought to the white space of the page. The third part,* Leteo, *is a voyage through the river of memory. To sip this water is to lose one's fear of dying, of going unrecalled.* Leteo *is a thinking landscape, and it is the return from darkness and oblivion.*

Desde SHAJARIT

En las migraciones de los claveles rojos donde revientan cantos de
aves picudas y se pudren las manzanas antes del desastre
Ahí donde las mujeres se palpan los senos y se tocan el sexo
en el sudor de los polvos de arroz y de la hora del té
Flujo de enredaderas a través de lo que siempre es lo mismo
Ciudades atravesadas por el pensamiento
Miércoles de ceniza
La vieja nana nos mira a través de un haz de luz
Respiran estanques de sombras, llueve morados casi rojos
¿Arriba es abajo?
Estamos en la fragilidad de la corteza del otoño
En el parque rectangular
en la canícula cuando los colores claros son los más conmovedores
Después de Shajarit
olvidadas plegarias, ásperas
Nacen vientos levemente aclarados por la oración, bosques de pirules
Y mi abuela tocaba siempre la misma sonata
Una niña toma una nieve en la esquina de una calle soleada
Un hombre lee un periódico mientras espera el camión
Se fractura la luz
Una pareja de mediana edad todavía se atreve a tomarse de la mano
Y la ropa está tendida al sol. Impenetrable la sonata de la abuela

From SHAJARIT

Editor's note: Instituted by Abraham, who rose early, Shajarit is a daily early morning
prayer and the longest prayer of the day. It includes benediction, psalms, shema, and
amidah.

In the migrations of red carnations, where the songs of the long-billed
      birds
break and the apples rot, before the disaster:
There where the women fondle their breasts and finger their sex
in the moisture of makeup and the hour for tea
Flow of vines across what stays always the same
Cities entangled in thinking
Wednesday as of ashes
The old nanny watches us through a countenance of light
Shadow-pools exhale, seeping a purple that is nearly red
The heat rubs its muzzle
Downstairs, the street is flooded by the moon
We are poised on the delicate cusp of autumn
In the rectangular park
in the dog days when the clearest colors are the most poignant
After Shajarit
forgotten prayers, raw
Breezes lightly rise, cleansed by invocations, forests of alders
And my grandmother played the same sonata over and over
A girl clutches a cup of shaved ice in the slanted alley light
A man reads a newspaper while waiting for the bus
The light breaks into pieces

Tú dijiste que era el verano. Oh música
Y la invasión de las albas y la invasión de los verdes
Abajo, gritos de niños que juegan, vendedores de nueces
respiración de rosas amarillas
Y mi abuela me dijo a la salida del cine
sueña que es hermoso el sueño de la vida, muchacha

En el vértigo de Kol Nidrei antes de comenzar el gran ayuno
En los vapores azules de las sinagogas
Después y antes de Rosh Hashaná
En el color blanco de la lluvia en la Plaza del Carmen
mi abuela rezando el rosario de las cinco
y tus oscuros antiquísimos ojos niña de siempre
El eco del Shofar abre el año

♦

En la crecida de los ríos
En la noche de los sauces
cuando más te amo
en los lavaderos del sueño desde donde se desprende ese vaho de
entrañas femeninas inconfundible y anchuroso
Te dejo mi muerte íntegra, intacta, absolutamente virgen
toda mi muerte para ti
¿A quién se habla antes de morir? ¿dónde estás?
¿en qué parte de mí puedo inventarte?

♦

    Todo no es sino tiempo
Allá donde unas cuantas bugambilias en un vaso de agua
bastan para hacernos un jardín
Porque morimos solos. Y la muerte es apenas el despertar
de este sueño primero de vivir y dijo mi abuela a la salida del cine
sueña que es hermoso el sueño de la vida, muchacha
Se oxida la lumbre de las veladoras

A middle-aged couple moves to take each other's hands
And a veil spreads over the sun. Impenetrable, my grandmother's sonata

It is summer, you said.
Oh music
And the invasion of whiteness and the invasion of green
Beneath, cries of the children at play, the peanut vendors,
Yellow roses breathing
As we leave the movies my grandmother tells me
Dream that it is lovely, muchacha —the dream of life

In the vertigo of the Kol Nidrei, after the fasting has begun
In the synagogue's blue hazes
Then and after Rosh Hashanah
In the whiteness of rain in the Plaza del Carmen
my grandmother praying the rosary at five in the afternoon
The echo of the Shofar saturates the year

♦

In the swelling of the rivers
In the willows' night
when I love you most
in the cleansing dream, when this breath
from the female depths dissolves—unmistakable, set-loose—
I offer you my death—whole, intact,
all my death for you
Whom am I going to talk with, in the face of dying? Where are you?
In what part of me can I invent you?

♦

Life is nothing but time:
Where a few sprigs of bougainvillea in a vase of water
are enough—we have a garden!

y yo, ¿dónde estoy?
Soy la que fui siempre. Lo inesperado de estar siendo
Llego al lugar del principio donde comienza el comienzo
Este es el tiempo
Es el tiempo de despertar
La abuela enciende las velas sabáticas desde su muerte y me mira
Se extiende el sábado hasta nunca, hasta después, hasta antes
Mi abuela que murió de sueños
mece interminablemente el sueño que la inventa
que yo invento. Una niña loca me mira desde adentro

Estoy intacta

Because we die alone. And because death is enough to awaken us
from this first dream of living, and as we left the movies my grandmother
  said
Dream that it is lovely, muchacha—the dream of life
The candle flame rusts
and I, where am I?
I am what continues forever. The surprise of being
I am back to the place of origin, where beginnings begin
This is the time
It is the time of awakening
The old woman lights her Sabbath candles from her death and she watches
  me
The Sabbath expands till never, till after, till before
My grandmother who died of dreams
endlessly stirs the dream that she invented
and I invent. A wild girl watches me from my inmost self

I am intact

Translated by Stephen Tapscott

Desde YISKOR

57.

¿Me oyes? Debajo de mi nombre estoy yo
La pequeña olvidada dice que no sabe   dice que no sabe

Loba ¿estás allí?

Y para recordarme vuelvo a ti
Qué sola debes sentirte

(esto es sólo el testimonio del oyente)

59.

Escucho a través de paredes subterráneas como los presos se dan señales
unos a otros
Memoria ¿me oyes?
Creces como lo que se olvida
Y aquella que soy ofrece perdón a la que fui

▼▼▼

From YISKOR

Author's note: *Yiskor* derives from the Hebrew root *zajor,* which I take to mean "to remember," as in the prayer that begins "Remember, O Lord, the soul that has passed on to eternal life." The *Yiskor* is recited only four times a year.

57.

Can you hear me? under my name I am
The little lost one says she does not know   does not know
                                      She-wolf: are you there?
To remember I turn to you
What a loneliness you must feel
                       (This is only the testimony of the one who listens)

59.

I listen through underground walls like prisoners signaling
To one another
               Memory: can you hear me?
You grow, like some forgotten thing
And what I am forgives what I have been

60.

Sobre la mesa unas fotografías
Esa muchacha la de la izquierda al frente sí, esa soy yo

61.

El corazón
                Cráter
Testigo
      Contesta
                Contéstame
La voz pálida
          Cae
Las palabras desfondadas
              Caen
Inscripciones
          Fechas
Las muertes y lo que de ellas nace
                      No expliques
Perdida en ti
            Tú
                No expliques
Cada año
        Yiskor

63.

        Ella llora
        Sin tocarla en un acto reflejo lloro con ella
            Busco el lugar del corazón

Los gritos se pierden en lo oscuro del sueño   en la oscuridad de la noche
en lo oscuro de la casa   en la opacidad del silencio
La mañana se sostiene por las paredes verde pálido
Somos los que se van

60.

On the table a few photographs
That girl on the left in the front—it's me alright

61.

The heart
                    A crater
Witness
        Corroborate
                    Corroborate me
The pale voice
                Falls
The bottomless words
                    Fall
Inscriptions
                Dates
The deaths and what they gave birth to
                                You do not explain
Whatever was lost in you
                You
                        You do not explain
Each year
            Yiskor

63.

            She is crying
        In a sudden impulse, I too cry with her
                I am searching for the heart's space

The weeping is lost in the dark of the dream   in the darkness of night
in the dark of the house   in the opacity of silence
The morning holds to the pale green walls
We are the ones leaving

68.

Desembarcamos un mediodía en el puerto de Veracruz. Traímos abrigos gruesos
de piel. En La Habana comí mango por primera vez ¿A quién contarle esto?

Memoria del mar y su tedio, de la muchacha que fui. El vestido gris que ahora se
ve ridículo en la fotografía. Memoria de las tablas percudidas del barco, de aquellas
olas impávidas, caducas en su belleza Memoria de la luna casi insoportable

Es mediodía. Es hoy. Desembarco. Es un día de agosto
Jamás me había sentido tan aferrada a la vida

73.

Ella se arranca de su sombra. Es una mujer vieja y sigue siendo hermosa. Las
palabras no la alcanzan. Su piel ha sido devastada por la falta de caricias. Tampoco
hay ruido. La vida es el único refugio. Estar aquí para nadie. Para nada. Ah, cómo
te moriste en mí

74.

La tierra se deshiela. No sé por qué esta mañana me quedará para siempre. Es el
olor de los lirios arrancádose a la nieve (en realidad es una mañana igual a las
demás) ¿Por qué es ésta la que guardo?

75.

Una mujer con un vestido gris. Un recuerdo apenas para unos cuantos que
acabarán por olvidarla. Algunas tardes compartidas que se asemejarán a otras, los
crepúsculos, la mañana de un día caluroso. Tercos sueños, dádivas para nadie
apenas para ella misma. La fotografía no nos descubre nada, (todavía es una mujer
joven). Yo nunca la conocí

68.

We'd dock at noon in the port of Veracruz. We'd wear our Russian furs. In Havana I tasted a mango for the first time. Who can recount all this?

Memories of the sea and its weariness, of the girl I was. The gray dress that seems so preposterous now in the photo. Memory of the stained boards of the boat, impervious to waves, perishable in its beauty. Memory of the moon—nearly unendurable.

It is noon. It is today. I dock. It is an August day I have never felt so anchored in my life

73.

She detaches herself from her shadow. She is an old woman and still beautiful. Words do not reach her. Her skin has already been damaged by the lack of caresses. Soon it will be ruined completely. Life is the only refuge. To be here for nobody. For nothing. Oh, how can you have died inside me!

74.

The earth thaws. I do not know why this morning lingers forever. It is the smell of irises sprung from the snow (actually it is a morning like any other). Why do I brood over this one?

75.

The woman in a gray dress. Barely a memory, for the few who will finally forget her. Lengthened, some evenings that look like any other. Dawn of a hot day. Difficult dreams, gifts for nobody, much less for her. The photograph yields no clues (she's still a young woman). I never knew her.

76.

           Aquella muchacha sola en el muelle
                     Esta imagen para siempre
        ¿Qué vida fue ésta?
                 ¿Y qué es lo que esto quiere decir?

Mi voz se confunde con la tuya
El verano se desborda   los pájaros se golpean contra la luz

Y yo no puedo despertar

80.

El silencio es un trabajo que durará toda su vida. Ocurre en lo más
profundo, en lo más oscuro como una enfermedad mortal

¿Yo? ¿Esa mujer soy yo?

83.

     Nada   no me dices nada
           Tú que me escuchas
           La hora del dolor ha pasado

     Nada   no queda nada
           Tú que me escuchas ¿todavía reconoces a la que fui?
           Soy yo la que puede morir en cualquier momento

           El tedio de la espera
el diagrama de la lluvia   el movimiento de los sueños
           el pasto cubierto de hojas secas

76.

> This girl alone on the pier
> > This eternal image
> What life was that?
> > And what might this mean?

My voice mingles with yours
The summer overflows   birds throw themselves against the light

And I cannot waken

80.

Silence is a task that will last all her life. It continues
in the depths, in the darkness, like a mortal illness

And I? Am I that woman?

83.

> Nothing   you tell me nothing
> > You who are listening for me
> > The grieving-time is over

> Nothing   absolutely nothing remains
> > You who are listening for me, Do you still recognize
> > who I was? I who could die at any moment

> > The tedium of hope
> the diagram of the rain   the motion of dreams
> > the lawn littered with dry leaves

▼▼

85.

Acaso somos la misma oscuridad   las mismas palabras   los mismos gritos
                     Nunca lo sabrás   Los muertos no entienden a los vivos

                          Y si fuera hasta tus fauces
                     Y si fuera hasta el remordimiento
                        Tú que ya no me escuchas
                       Tú que ya no me oyes llorar
                 Abreme el perdón   acógeme en tu indiferencia

La tierra te ha deshecho
No sabes que estoy aquí
      La lluvia arrecia   Se parte como las aguas del Estigia
      Nada que temer   Somos cómplices
                         no te debo nada   concédeme tu olvido

                         ¿Donde está tu muerte ahora?

87.

                    ¿Y qué buscabas en aquel sueño?
Ten piedad de aquellos que ya han vivido su vida
Dame la añoranza para que pueda buscarte en lo profundo de las cisternas
Todo cuanto he amado desapareció
                         Estoy cercada
                         Ruega por mí

85.

Maybe we are the same darkness   the same words   the same cries
        You'll never know it   The dead do not comprehend the living

                        And if it came to your very jaws
                          And if it came to remorse
                        You who no longer listen for me
                        You who no longer hear my cries
        Hold out some mercy for me   Shelter me in your indifference

The earth has undone you
You do not know I am here
        The rain falls harder   It opens like the waters of the Styx.
        Fear nothing   We are accomplices
                            I owe you nothing   grant me your oblivion

                            Where is your death now?

87.

                        And what were you searching for, in that dream?
Have mercy, for those who lived their lives
Grant me the aching to search for you through the depth of wells
All I have loved has vanished
                        I am walled in
                        Pray for me

Translated by Stephen Tapscott

Isabel Fraire

Isabel Fraire was born in Mexico City in 1934. She has been actively publishing poetry, criticism, and translations for thirty years. *Seis poetas de lengua inglesa* (SEP/Setentas), Fraire's translations of Pound, Eliot, cummings, Stevens, Auden, and W. C. Williams, was published in Mexico in 1976. Two years later, the third book of her own poetry, *Poemas en el regazo de la muerte,* appeared and was awarded the Villaurrutia Prize. Thomas Hoeksema has translated this book, *Poems in the Lap of Death* (Latin American Literary Review Press, 1981) and an earlier book, *Poems* (Mundus Artium Press). Isabel Fraire lives in London with her husband and surviving son.

◆

I had two sons. The eldest died last year. His name was David Montano Fraire and he died of cancer, of sheer neglect, in a psychiatric ward. This happened in Puebla, Mexico, and I was with him for the last two years. He was a fine painter and would have been one of the best. I intend to write a book about him, because it needs to be written, but find myself unable to do it yet. He was thirty-three years old. My other son, Rolando Montano Fraire, a keen musician and computer whiz, is determined to become a psychiatrist or a psychologist or something of the sort. He lives in Mexico City.

As for my translations, how I learned English: the answer is that my Canadian grandmother lost her husband and came down to live with us in Mexico City when I was three. She was wonderful, and she taught me to read before I went to school. She never learned Spanish at all, though she tried. So I had to learn English and go around with her to shops, interpreting. My mother was American and my father Mexican, but I always felt myself to be, and am, a Mexican. I lived in Mexico and went to the States only as an adult. I did have a bicultural education though and read Shakespeare all the way through about the same time I read El Quijote all the way through. I liked Shakespeare better.

Ever since I first started publishing poetry, I have been asked to articulate my aesthetics: what is poetry for? what am I trying to do by writing it? is it of any earthly use? My personal biography was of no interest to my Mexican readers who couldn't care less whether I was 88 or 16, hetero- or homosexual, a clandestine mother or otherwise. What they wanted to know was my philosophy of poetry. A bit later, when I started giving readings, there was always some member of the audience who asked, rather aggressively, what I thought of political poetry, and whether poets should not put their poetry in the service of some higher cause, such as the welfare of the people, instead of simply stroking their egos in obscure language that nobody could understand.

I think poetry, like art, teaches us to see, opens our eyes to what exists around us. The poet, like the artist, points at something that is there, outside himself, so that others can perhaps see it and share the vision, or rejoice in seeing their own visions confirmed, set out in words or colors, for all to see. My only reason for writing is to grasp that moment of awareness and somehow to leave it there, outside me, in readiness for any who wish to share it.

With regard to the political purpose of poetry, I believe the question is answered by referring to impulse and language. The poet picks up the language around him and makes it his own. A poet does not set out to say things in an incomprehensible way, he only listens to the language he hears inside his head. And, if he is a good poet, even though difficult, others learn his language and are enriched by it, as in the case of Gongora or Pound. However, the idea that any language is inaccessible is in itself elitist. The poet must follow not his muse but certainly his inclination. If he wants to write about Nelson Mandela or Che Guevara or about a strike or about the contents of his refrigerator some people will be turned off, but that cannot stop him.

I am well aware that I keep saying him, or his, when referring to the poet. That is not because I am under the impression all poets are men, but only because I find it cumbrous to say his or her poem each time. Which leads me to consider the present ghettoization of literature by gender, politics, race, and nationality. Often, women are expected to write about feminist issues; if they don't, their work is questioned, they are regarded as insensitive or as cowards, aspirants to a male sensibility. The same is true of gay or third-world writers who are expected to similarly limit their point of view. In any of these cases, the writers are not taken as seriously as they would be if they were intellectual, first-world, male, heterosexual writers who are privileged to deal with any and all issues from that detached, superior point of view whereby all serious discussions and debates take place. The only reason Latin American authors of the boom were taken seriously was because, in the beginning, they had some very articulate, English-speaking, European travelers as their spokesmen. Carlos Fuentes, Julio Cortazar, and Octavio Paz, for instance, gained fairly universal respect for what they had to say of their work and of their contemporaries. Borges was admired on his own account, but I have a slippery suspicion that it was because he was seen as a science fiction writer.

One more thing. I consider each poem as an end in itself, with a shape of its own. As what I want to say changes, so does the language I use, so does the shape. It all hinges on what I am trying to say. I only put poems together in book form with great effort. They are individual acts. However, they do seem to fit.

MOMENTO DE UN DIA DEL SIGLO DIECIOCHO INMOVILIZADO POR UN PINTOR JAPONES VISTO EN UN MOMENTO DEL SIGLO VEINTE EN UNA GALERIA LONDINENSE

un pájaro gordo
negro
no especialmente bello
con las plumas de la cabeza erizadas por el frío
o por el viento
se agarra con fuerza de una rama casi vertical

por su postura se adivina
que la rama es mecida por el viento

el pájaro
mira
con sus pequeños ojos negros
parecidos a semillas
o botones

algo
que está fuera del cuadro
y nosotros no vemos

A MOMENT CAPTURED BY A JAPANESE PAINTER
OF THE EIGHTEENTH CENTURY
SEEN IN A MOMENT OF THE TWENTIETH CENTURY
IN A LONDON GALLERY

a plump black
bird
not very attractive
head feathers bristling
from cold
or wind
forcefully clings to
a nearly vertical branch

his posture tells us
that the branch
is being stirred by the wind

the bird
stares
with small black eyes
like seeds
or buttons
at something
outside the scene
we cannot see

Translated by Thomas Hoeksema

SIN TÍTULO

en cuanto sale el sol

    todo sale sobrando

        basta
            con abrir los ojos
          desperezarse
          como un gato

y todo lo demás
    los sistemas
        filosóficos
            políticos
    las profundas disquisiciones
        éticas
          estéticas

son sólo
    una manera agradable de pasar el rato
bellos garigoleos barrocos de los cuales hay que regresar
      para recuperar
        aquí en el sol
      el goce simple de la propia piel

UNTITLED

the minute the sun comes out

    everything is beside the point

        it is enough
                to open your eyes
            to stretch your limbs
            like a cat

and all the rest
    philosophical
        political
                systems
    deep moral and
        aesthetic
           disquisitions

are only
    a pleasant means of whiling away the time
beautiful baroque flourishes from which you must retreat
      to recover
        here in the sun
      the simple pleasure of your
                      own
                        skin

Translated by Thomas Hoeksema

SIN TÍTULO

creo que el tiempo

gira

lenta

más lentamente

y se detiene

ahora

y estamos

en el sol   sobre el pasto

y   alrededor

cada   cosa   que   miro

también   está   estando

UNTITLED

time

revolves

slowly

slower yet

and   pauses

and we are

here

now

in the sun   on the grass

and

around   us

each thing we see

is here now

Translated by Thomas Hoeksema

"COMPLEJO HABITACIONAL"

I.

la mañana surge lentamente como un vapor que se eleva
            y se difunde en el aire

cruza   los cuadros de verde pasto
    saltando   corriendo   saltando
            un niño
                con una bolsa de mandado en la mano

II.

los edificios de departamentos
                    presentan superficies planas   rectangulares

        las ventanas tienen contraventanas grises
            que se cierran   o abren
                    como tapas
                            cada cuarto una caja

el jardín   de pasto liso y verde como alfombra recién comprada
        está encuadrado por filas regulares de árboles idénticos
            que arrojan una sombra continua
                como la de un muro

"HOUSING COMPLEX"

I.

morning rises slowly like a mist climbing
                and spreading through the air

a child crosses   squares of green grass
        running   jumping   running
                carrying
                        a shopping bag in its hand

II.

the apartment buildings
                present flat rectangular   surfaces

        the windows are equipped with gray steel shutters
                that close   or open
                        like lids
                                each room a box

the garden   of smooth green grass   like a new carpet
        is framed by regular rows of identical trees
                that cast an oblong shadow
                        like a wall

III.

aquí nadie se habla   me dice una vecina
              que después de un año
                          ha roto con la regla
a horas previsibles
                          dos o tres viejos   y una niña
                              sacan a pasear sus respectivos perros
                      uno de ellos acostumbra
                                      soltarle la cadena
                      los otros se detienen
                                  cada vez
                                              que se detiene el perro

IV.

en general reina el silencio
                          sólo roto por el ruido del tráfico
                      que aumenta notoriamente
                          a las horas de entrada y salida de las oficinas

pero ocasionalmente
              se oye   a través de las paredes
                      una discusión agria   violenta
                              cargada del resentimiento
                          de una vida estropeada
              o la música de fondo
                                  melodramática y jadeante
                      de la televisión

V.

a una cuadra de distancia
              grandes máquinas

III.

no one speaks to each other here   a neighbor tells me
        breaking the rule
                        after a year
at predetermined hours
                two or three old men and a child
                        take their respective dogs out for a walk
                one of them is in the habit of
                                letting the dog run loose
                the others stop
                        each time
                                the dog stops

IV.

usually silence prevails
                        broken only by the noise of traffic
                that swells
                        at the hours when offices open or close

but occasionally
        through paper-thin walls   one overhears
                a bitter violent   discussion
                                full of resentment
                        for a ruined life
                melodramatic panting
                                background music
                        from the television set

V.

a block away
        large bulldozers

se ocupan de arrasar un bosquecillo

para levantar un gran conjunto de edificios
   idénticos a éste

busily demolish a small grove

in order to erect a mass of buildings
        exactly like this one

Translated by Thomas Hoeksema

MEDIODIA

se desdobla uno infinitamente
            para verse
y en este desdoblarse
        pierde la imagen

el espejo de cara ante el espejo

◆

hemos roto el día en dos mitades de naranja
una para nadie y la otra para nadie
y nosotros en el centro, inmóviles,
            bañados por el sol

◆

nadie es sombra
        nadie es espejo
            el polvo de sol se dispersa ocupándolo todo

◆

en el centro del día
        me convierto en nada
a mis ojos acuden objetos
        colmados de presencia

NOON

In order to see
        one is infinitely revealed
and in this revelation
            the image is lost

the mirror-face before the mirror

◆

we have separated day into two halves of an orange
one part for no one and the other for no one
and we are in the center, motionless,
                cleansed by the sun

◆

no one is shadow
        no one is mirror
            the sun's dust scatters
                attracted to everything

◆

in the center of day
        I am transformed into nothing
    objects stir before my eyes

bañados en luz
    llenos de sí mismos

       ◆

por encima de los árboles
    el aire—lleno de luz

en la sombra cada cosa en su lugar
brizna tras brizna de pasto
arruga tras arruga de corteza

       filled with their own presence
purified by light
     full of themselves

   ◆

above the trees
    the air—full of light

in the shadows each thing in its place
blade after blade of grass
ridge after ridge of bark

Translated by Thomas Hoeksema

Elsa Cross

Elsa Cross was born in 1946. In 1972 she published her first volume of poetry, *La dama de la torre*, and it was awarded a national prize for younger poets (SEP). This was followed by *Tres Poemas* (1981) and *Bacantes* (1982). All three early books have been republished along with other poems in one volume, *Espejo al sol/Poesia 1964-1981* (SEP-Plaza y Valdes, 1989). Later books include *Baniano* (1986), *Canto Malabar* (1987), *El Divan de Antar* (1990)—winner of the National Poetry Prize "Aguacalientes"—and *Jaguar* (1991). She has been a fellow at the Mexican Center for Writers and the National Foundation for the Arts and a member of the International Writing Program at the University of Iowa.

She finished her doctoral studies in philosophy at the National Autonomous University of Mexico, writing her dissertation on Hindu philosophy, a subject she had studied in the United States and in India, where she lived for two years. In addition to having many of her poems published in translation in the United States and in Europe, she has written a book on Nietzsche's aesthetics, *La Realidad Transfigurada* (1985), and numerous essays. Elsa Cross works as a professor of Philosophy of Religion at the National Autonomous University of Mexico.

◆

When I was beginning to write, poetry was everything for me: a search, a way to express myself. It was what gave meaning to my life.

Later, at the root of my encounter with meditation and with my long stay in India, I began to lose my "identity" as a poet. What I believed poetry was faded out behind a more profound experience.

Nevertheless, poetry is always there, and it seems to surge independently from what I think or feel about it. It is also independent from external circumstances, literary styles, or ideologies. It seems to have its own life.

The Romantic poets considered themselves to be only instruments of the real creative force. This is also my sensation. And to feel oneself as a mere vehicle is liberating.

I believe what Heidegger said: Poetry is the foundation of the self through the word. That is the scope where I find it. Yet it isn't, in this sense, dissociated from the quotidian. On the contrary, it is revealed in the middle of all, because it is like that sphere whose center is everywhere and whose circumference is nowhere.

As time goes on, poetry and I become each other. It stops being only an activity or a literary task, and it becomes a constant perception, an inner sound, a way of loving life.

Desde CANTO MALABAR

III.

Grandes ciudades de piedra
dejaron sobre sus muros una historia cifrada.
Un río junta sus aguas a la tarde
cuando el aire parece desprederse de una sílaba.
Gaviotas volando a contramar
Sabor de herrumbre.
Ciudades que aguardan esa historia, la nuestra.
Grandes espacios mudos a nuestro canto.
Un río brilla bajo el crepúsculo,
viste su superficie de hojas de oro.

Los barcos a lo lejos.
Por el camino crecen araucarias.
Camino sin regreso.
El viento rompe unas guirnaldas de papel.
Suavemente serpentean listones blancos.
Como veo con los ojos cerrados
unos hilos de luz alzarse de mi cuerpo.

From CANTO MALABAR

Editor's note: Elsa Cross's book, *Canto Malabar,* from which parts III and IV are extracted and translated here, is prefaced by a brief statement explaining that this poem (which is comprised of seven parts) takes as its point of departure the Hindu legend of Savitri, in which the woman pursues her lover beyond death in order to save him.

III.

Great cities of rock
left an enciphered history upon their walls.
A river joins its waters to the evening
when the air seems to release a syllable.
Gulls flying counter-tide.
Taste of iron rust.
Cities that await this history, ours.
Great spaces silent to our song.
A river shines beneath the twilight,
adorns its surface with leaves of gold.

The boats in the distance.
Araucarias grow along the path.
Path without return.
The wind breaks paper garlands.
White ribbons snake gently.
As I see with closed eyes
threads of light rise from my body.

Exaltación—olvido.
Y no hay puerto cerrado a tu presencia.
Todo lo alcanza, todo lo envuelve, todo lo enciende.
Ay, memoria de ti.
Con la arena deslizándose bajo la ropa,
pegándose a los pies
entre medusas violáceas,
miro el sol que desciende
como quien llama a la Muerte
entre las hojas puntiagudas del acanto
y ve brillar pedazos de mármol
sobre la hierba seca.
Como quien invoca a la Muerte.

¿Y la Muerte qué?
Pequeñas mariposas volando entre las ruinas.
No hay medida del tiempo.
Las gaviotas se perfilan en línea al litoral.
Una ola se fuga por la orilla.
Miro el agua hundirse en las arenas,
y de pronto—sensación de la arena—
se deshace en el agua la conciencia del cuerpo.
Infinito es el ámbito.
La posesión ilimitada—

Y no hay más acontecer:
unas cuantas gaviotas mirando un mismo punto . . .

IV.

Dejé en la orilla mis sueños más amados.
Todo lo que se alzaba
en la marea del tiempo ya vivido,
lo que pedía al tiempo por venir.
Deseos esculpidos en la roca,

Exaltation—oblivion.
And there is no port closed to your presence.
Everything reaches, embodies, kindles.
Oh, memory of you.
With sand slipping away under your robe,
sticking to your feet
between violaceous medusas,
I watch the sun that descends
like one who calls to Death
between prickly leaves of the thistle
and who see pieces of marble shine
upon the dry grass.
Like one invoking Death.

And Death, what?
Little butterflies flying among the ruins.
There is no measure of time.
Gulls turn in line toward the coast.
A wave evanesces on the shore.
I watch the water sink into the sands,
and suddenly—sensation of sand—
consciousness of the body disappears in the water.
The scope is infinite.
The possession unlimited—

And there is nothing more to happen:
a few gulls looking at a same point . . .

IV.

I left my most beloved dreams on the shore.
Everything that rose
in the tide of time already lived,
what I asked of time to come.
Desires sculpted in rock,

sueños brillando como arrecifes bajo el sol,
sueños errando
en busca de un fin que desconocen.

De cara al tiempo
formas excavadas en la roca
dejaron el sedimento de las eras
penetrar por sus poros.
Mil años sumergidos,
al receder el agua dejó sobre los cuerpos
sus anillos calcáreos
a la altura del corazón;
mareas en las cavernas del sentido,
sentimientos ahogados.

Filo del tiempo,
escoplo,
hizo saltar toda la roca en torno
dejando intacto en lo oscuro
un deseo anudado,
botón que se marchita sin abrirse,
hálito en la piedra que no alcanza
a decir
el impulso de fuego que lo habita,

si una voz no se alza entre los muros
y hace reverberar una escala ignorada.
Repetida al final de centurias
vibra en la oreja de piedra,
arranca la escama endurecida.
Así tras de la boca de la cueva
silba el viento en los montes
arrebatando el polvo amarillo de las peñas,
cortezas amargas,
memoria de suelos sagrados . . .

dreams shining like reefs under the sun,
dreams wandering
in search of an unknown end.

Facing time
forms carved in rock
left the sediment of ages
to penetrate through its pores.
A thousand submerged years,
receding, water left on the bodies
its calcareous rings
at the height of the heart;
tides in the caverns of feeling,
feelings drowned.

Blade of time,
chisel,
it broke the rock into pieces
leaving intact in the darkness
a knotted desire,
a bud that withers without opening,
breath in the rock that does not
give voice
to the impulse of fire that inhabits it,

if a voice does not rise between the walls
and make a forgotten scale reverberate.
Repeated to the end of centuries
it vibrates in the ear of stone,
it strips the hardened scales.
Thus beyond the mouth of the cave
the wind whistles in the hills
stirring the yellow dust of the cliffs,
bitter tree barks
memory of sacred grounds . . .

Estupas en ruinas.
Campanarios derruidos y su silencio
al ángelus del alba.
Memoria de estrellas rotas,
holocaustos.
Leones alados custodiando un recinto vacío.
El fuego se extinguió,
el viento dispersó las profecías
y ahora se oyen
sólo sordos reptiles entre el polvo.

Cae el crepúsculo
incendiando el último reflejo de esa luz
—eco de un nombre que se pierde
cuando la luna cambia de faz.
Juega el sol en la hierba todavía,
hace danzar al aire chupamirtos.
La mirada se mira a sí misma,
traspasa el velo
que oculta tu refulgencia en cada cosa.

Allí estás tú, que te fugas del tiempo.
Tú, a quien se nombra
como el principio, el medio y el fin,
como el sendero y la puerta,
como la cima,
como el relámpago.
Allí estás tú, aunque aparezcan
los rebaños de cabras,
las gavillas,
mujeres que aplanan el suelo de su era.

◆

Del brillo de tus pies
se alza una ola de luz,

Shrines in ruins.
Razed belfries and their silence
at the Angelus of dawn.
Memory of broken stars,
holocausts.
Winged lions guarding an empty precinct.
The fire extinguished,
the wind dispersed the prophecies
and now only deaf reptiles
are heard among the dust.

Twilight falls
kindling the last reflection of that light
—echo of a name that is lost
when the moon changes phase.
The sun still plays in the grass,
it makes hummingbirds dance in the air.
The gaze watches itself,
pierces the veil
that hides your radiant glow in each thing.

There you are, who flees time.
You who is named
as the beginning, the middle and the end,
as the path and the door,
as the summit,
as the lightning flash.
There you are, even though
herds of goats appear,
sheafs of grain,
women who flatten the ground of their threshing-floor.

◆

From the shine of your feet
a wave of light rises,

como si caminaras sobre el agua,
como si ascendieras al cielo en su relámpago.
Se vuelven los pies de cada dios,
de Shánkara y de Gauri
—Shiva de las mil formas—,
de Allah sin figura,
del Uno perdido en los sepulcros de Amarna,
de Yahveh en el desierto.

Dios ebrio en los bosques rompiendo toda ley.
Dios dictando preceptos desde sus hipogeos.
Dios de los justos y de los impíos.
Dios de los necios y de los sensatos.
Dios tomando ser
en toda cosa que vive y respira sobre la tierra,
en todo lo que existe
y en todo lo que no existe.
Dios que deja sin fin fluir su gracia
mientras una mujer
le envuelve los pies en sus cabellos—

Pies dorados como lotos.
En octubre se iban los cuclillos,
la hierba se secaba sobre el campo.
Lotos floreciendo por todas partes,
en las charcas que dejaron las lluvias,
en las pilas de agua, en los estanques.
Guirnaldas dondequiera.
Y cuando tú te fuiste
cómo llenó su aroma tus recintos.
"Y tu ensueño se enreda en mi cabello . . ."

A la sombra más fresca de tu patio
silencio del cuenco de tus manos
como agua bebí.
Follajes jaspeados,

as if you were walking on water,
as if you were ascending to the sky in its flash.
Your feet become the feet of each god,
of Shankara and of Gauri
—Shiva of a thousand forms—,
of Allah without a face,
of the One lost in the sepulchres of Amarna,
of Yahweh in the desert.

God drunk in the forests breaking all law.
God dictating precepts from his hypogea.
God of the righteous and of the impious.
God of the foolish and the wise.
God taking form
in all things that live and breathe on earth,
in all that exists
and in all that does not exist.
God who lets his grace flow without end
while a woman
covers his feet with her hair—

Feet golden as lotus flowers.
In October the cuckoos left,
the grass dried in the field.
Lotus flowers flourishing everywhere,
in the pools left by the rains,
in the fonts of water, in the ponds.
Garlands everywhere.
And when you left
how his aroma filled your precincts.
"And your reverie becomes entangled in my hair . . . "

In the freshest shade of your patio
I drank silence like water
from the bowl of your hands.
Sparkling foliage,

muscarias alargaban la tarde
picoteando entre el bambú.
El viento sepultaba la hierba
bajo tantas buganvilias que hacía caer
desde la enredadera,
la adornaba como un lecho de bodas—

Cámaras mortuorias, cámaras nupciales
bajo la inclinación de un ángulo cerrado,
absorbiendo en un punto de fuga
la fuerza
de tu nombre mismo que se invoca
hacia la luna nueva.
Así fui perdiendo parte a parte
mi cuerpo todo,
y en tu ausencia completa
sólo quedó un fantasma de mí misma.

flycatchers prolonged the afternoon
pecking among the bamboo.
The wind buried the grass
under so many bougainvillae that it shook
from the vine,
grass adorned like a marriage bed—

Mortuary chambers, nuptial chambers
under the inclination of a closed angle,
absorbing in a vanishing point
the force
of your very name that is invoked
toward the new moon.
In this way I was losing
my whole body
part by part,
and in your complete absence
only a phantom remained of myself.

Translated by Jenny Goodman and Ofelia Ferran

Elva Macías

Elva Macías's work has been anthologized both in Mexico and in the
United States, where she has lectured in colleges and universities
throughout the southwest. In 1971 she won a scholarship from the
Mexican Center for Writers. Her books include *El paso del que viene, Circulo
del Sueno, Imagen y Semejanza,* and *Pasos Contados.* Her newest collection of
poems is *Lejos de la Memoria,* and her most recent projects include two
books of poems, one of which is for children—something she has wanted
to do for a long time.

◆

*I was born on January 10, 1944, in Tuxtla Gutierrez, capital of the state of
Chiapas, because my mother delivered her three children in that city. But forty days
after my birth, we moved to our town, Villaflores, which was founded by my maternal
great-grandfather in 1873, during the anti-reelection struggles. On both sides my
family is closely united with the history of that place. My only ancestor who wrote is
my maternal grandfather, a popular poet, author of* Himno a Chiapas, *martyred
during the 1913 Revolution. I've kept his original notebooks, some portraits, and an
idealized image of him because I was growing up in a world concerned with commerce
and livestock.*

*I studied in my province and in Mexico City in religious schools; in one of them I
met the writer Elsa Cross with whom even today I maintain a constant professional
and friendly dialogue. In 1963, after an engagement of three days, I married the
writer Eraclio Zepeda, and we went to live in the People's Republic of China where
he was a professor of Hispano-American literature and where I gave Spanish classes to
eight- and nine-year-olds.*

*In 1964 we moved to the Soviet Union. My only daughter, Masha, was born
there. I studied Russian in the State University of Moscow and my husband was a
press correspondent. On returning to Mexico, in 1968, I began my first job as
coordinator of expositions in the Department of Plastic Arts in the National Institute
of Fine Arts. There I began a long professional involvement in the promotion and
diffusion of culture in this institute, in the National Autonomous University of
Mexico, and in my native state. Now I direct the Museum of the National University*

of Chopo, a center that offers the public multidisciplinary cultural activities, being the principal center for exhibits by contemporary artists.

Like many women who are mothers, I have divided my time between domestic tasks, the pleasures of seeing my daughter grow and mature (now she is a young painter), my work at the university, and the hours dedicated to writing. I have never fought in feminist organizations, although I have always had a close relationship with the women with whom I live and with the concerns of women in my country. I know and I am interested in what my women colleagues write. As for my historic roots, I continue to promote the cultural diversity in the state of Chiapas; as an editor, I have published more than twenty titles by native and foreign authors on the history, the culture, and the literature of Chiapas.

As a writer, I come from that long literary tradition that has given the letters such national authors as Rosario Castellanos, Jaime Sabines, Juan Banuelos, Oscar Oliva, and Eraclio Zepeda, a tradition that is continuing with my generation and with the voices of younger poets.

NOSTALGIA

Girasol
que aun arrancado de su tallo
sigue atento al desplazamiento del sol.

NOSTALGIA

The sunflower
even torn from its stalk
still follows, attentive, the movement of the sun.

Translated by Henry Gerfen, Patricia Goedicke,
and Pilar Pinar Larrubia

ESTANCIAS

I.

Llegaste en busca de reposo
y tus ojos hallaron un espejo,
entre ellos y la imagen:
la deriva.

III.

El balcón enmarca las ramas del ciprés,
un insecto se desliza
por el aspa del ventilador
y el mosquitero es una pequeña nube
que se derrama sobre el deseo.

IV.

A la orilla del mar
habían milicianos
que no dejaban suicidarse
a los atribulados.

STANZAS

I.

You came looking for rest
and your eyes found a mirror,
between them and the image:
wandering.

III.

The balcony frames the branches of the cypress,
an insect slips
through the blades of the fan
and the mosquito net is a small cloud
spilling over desire.

IV.

At the edge of the sea
there were soldiers
who would not let the tormented
kill themselves.

V.

Única ave posible en el invierno,
el cuervo se regocija
con la inminencia del veranillo
antes del deshielo.

VII.

La brisa aparta las cortinas,
besa los caracoles marinos
que detienen las puertas de par en par.
Te adormece.
Sobre la tarde
tu sueño
es el mismo de ayer
y casi ríes.

X.

La limpia forma
de su belleza
se aleja
despojada de su aliento
de su culpa
suspendida en la tarde
se difuma
cada vez más paisaje.

V.

The only possible winter bird,
the crow rejoices
at the approaching summer
before the thaw.

VII.

The breeze parts the curtains,
kisses sea snails
that keep their doors wide open.
It lulls you.
Over the afternoon
your dream
is the same as yesterday
and you almost laugh.

X.

The clean shape
of your beauty
moves away
stripped of its breath
of its guilt
suspended in the afternoon
it fades
more and more into the landscape.

Translated by Henry Gerfen, Patricia Goedicke,
and Pilar Pinar Larrubia

LOS PASOS DEL QUE VIENE

I.

Danza nocturna de cascos en la piedra,
el joven Wang
cabalga con la lanza de su padre
a la primera cacería.
Ah, tal es su suerte,
cacería inicial:
un jabalí de presa
y el murmullo del grillo.

VIII.

En el brocal del pozo
suavemente doblé mi cuerpo.
Olor de insectos es el pozo,
tan sólo dije ah . . .
y la humedad arrebató mi voz.

XII.

Escribo a Chan Min Shu
un poema de despedida.
Pekín está cubierto de nieve,

THE STEPS OF THE ONE WHO COMES

I.

Night dance of hooves on stone,
the young Wang
rides with his father's lance
to his first hunt.
Ah, such luck,
his first time:
a wild boar for prey
and the murmuring of crickets.

VIII.

Over the mouth of the well
I leaned gently.
The well is the smell of insects.
I said only ah . . .
and the dampness took away my voice.

XII.

I write Chan Min Shu
a poem to say good-bye.
Peking is covered by snow,

ella pinta perdices;
las perdices escriben en la nieve.

XIII.

Interrumpieron mi labor
mínimos matices
modificando el tedio.
Desde mi regazo
las cuentas se dispersaron,
rodaron hasta la ofrenda última del día:
de inciensos y oraciones
cubro su partida,
se torne seda la muralla
a su paso,
notas de dulzaína
su regreso.

XV.

Ceremonia al despertar el año.
Ruido agotador de cigarras prisioneras
anuncia los pasos del que viene.
De estandartes y signos precedido,
precedido también de sacerdotes y letrados;
capitanes bajo la sombra púrpura del palio.
En ese prisma del tiempo,
en esa furia
marcada de batallas,
su figura se mueve
con el paso suntuoso
de un pavo real a punto de iniciar la danza:
Tsao-Tsao, general y señor de las cosechas
y el buen vino.

she paints partridges;
the partridges write on the snow.

XIII.

Tiny variations in color
interrupted my labor,
easing the boredom.
From my lap
the beads scattered,
rolling up to the day's last offering:
I cover your departure
with incense and prayers,
may the wall turn silk
at your passing,
notes of dulcimer
your return.

XV.

Ceremony for the awakening of the year.
An exhausting noise of imprisoned grasshoppers
announces the steps of the one who comes.
Preceded by banners and signs,
preceded, too, by priests and scholars;
captains under the purple shade of the canopy.
In that prism of time,
in that rage
marked with the seal of battles,
his figure moves
with the sumptuous step
of a peacock about to dance:
Tsao-Tsao, general and lord of harvests
and the good wine.

Translated by Henry Gerfen, Patricia Goedicke,
and Pilar Pinar Larrubia

HANSEL Y GRETEL

Guardamos las migajas del almuerzo,
las fuimos esparciendo una a una
en el camino,
la bruja nos condujo
de la mano
a la celda del incesto
y las hormigas
se ocuparon de borrar toda huella.

HANSEL AND GRETEL

We hoarded the crumbs from breakfast,
scattering them one by one
along the path,
the witch led us
by hand
to the prison of incest
while the ants
busied themselves erasing all traces.

Translated by Martha Christina

IMAGEN Y SEMEJANZA

El bien sea dado.
El mal no resucite.
Señora de la sentencia del ser,
es tu reino el que recorro
como el más humilde peregrino,
con la fe como báculo
y el azoro como único alimento.
Tu vía láctea se ensancha
cubierta de cercenaduras de estrellas
y el santuario aguarda únicamente tu determinación.
Mi esperanza se funda
en el entendimiento
de nuestra alcurnia y degradación
de nuestra virtud y nuestro vicio
de nuestro placer y atadura
de nuestra generosidad y rapiña.
¿A quién amamos?
Espejo de las miserias, dí,
espejo de la virtud,
explica.
Ya las cosechas no se pierden a nuestro paso
ni altar se erige sobre nuestro vientre.
Una es nuestra mano.
Una es la mano de la alianza,
una la que conduce los primeros pasos
de la progenie,

IMAGE AND LIKENESS

Let good be given.
Let evil not revive.
Woman, cursed into being,
it is your kingdom I travel
as the humblest pilgrim
with faith as a walking stick
and confusion the only food.
Your Milky Way widens
covered with cuttings of stars
and sanctuary awaits only
        your determination.
My hope is based
on the understanding
of our ascendence and degradation
of our virtue and our vice
of our pleasure and bonding
of our generosity and greed.
Whom do we love?
Mirror of miseries, speak,
mirror of virtue,
explain.
No longer are harvests ruined by our passing
nor an altar built upon our womb.
Our hand is one hand.
The single hand of alliance,
the one that directs the first steps

una la mano que se crispa
ante la esterilidad,
una la que rechaza la unión
la misma que arranca la constelación de la matriz
y la que recibe el astro de nuestro vientre.
No hay a quien culpar
no hay a quien agradecer.
Mujeres somos
desde el inicio de la gestación
hasta más allá de la vida y de la muerte
marcada o trunca en la estela de la descendencia.
Mujer también la que acompaña nuestros pasos
y exige el agua del deseo
el agua de la purificación
el agua de la inmundicia.
No sólo para incendiar la nave hemos nacido:
para tripular embarcaciones
que naufragarán con nuestra sola presencia,
para detener las furias del mar
con el pubis descubierto y salobre
como un mascarón de proa ante la tormenta.
Cese el canto de las sirenas
el llanto de mujeres castigadas
que se acostaron con ángeles del infierno.
Y no entre la nostalgia heredada
en nuestro lecho.
Nuestro lecho sea de paz
o de grandes batallas de placer,
nuestro lecho sea de soledad elegida.
El humo del sacrificio asciende
cuando la ofrenda es un animal enfermo
o el hijo más amado:
las prostitutas y las vírgenes
las madres y las yermas
las solas y las ayuntadas entre sí
las parejas fornicando

of children
one hand that convulses
against barrenness,   ·
one that rejects marriage
that same one that tears the constellation from the matrix
and that receives the star of our womb.
There is no one to blame
there is no one to thank.
We are women
from the beginning of gestation
to beyond life and death
branded or maimed on the pillar of origin.
Woman also the one who follows our steps
and demands the water of lust
the cleansing water
the water of lewdness.
We have come into the world
not only to set the ship on fire,
but to equip vessels
that shipwreck because of our presence alone,
to stop the furies of the sea
with the pubis exposed and salty
like a figurehead against the storm.
Stop the siren's song
the cry of chastened women
who slept with angels of hell.
And keep the inherited nostalgia
out of our bed.
Let our bed be peaceful
or the scene of great battles of pleasure,
or let the solitude we choose be our bed.
The smoke of sacrifice rises
when the offering is a sick animal
or the most loved son:
prostitutes and virgins
mothers and the barren

y los pequeños animales
domésticos que no quisimos ser.
Paraíso perdido
isla encantada
tierra de promisión
de tu entraña surge el volcán
que ha de sepultarnos.
Apartemos los vestigios
de todos los templos
mientras la luna se revierte
en el espejo de nuestro universo múltiple.

La manzana es de piedra
y latente está la semilla de la sierpe
que no ha de devorarse a sí misma.

the lonely and those united among themselves
the fornicating couples
and the small domestic
animals that we refused to be.
Paradise lost
enchanted island
promised land
from your entrails
surges the volcano
which will bury us.
Let us remove the remains
of all the temples
while the moon reverts
to the mirror of our multiple universe.

The apple is stone
and the seed of the serpent
that must not devour itself
is dormant.

Translated by Martha Christina

Verónica Volkow

Verónica Volkow lives in Mexico City. In 1980, Gabriel Zaid helped to establish Volkow's reputation by including a selection of her poems in his anthology of younger writers, *Asamblea de poetas jovenes de Mexico* (Siglo Veintiuno Editores). Her first substantial book, *Litoral de Tinta*, was published in 1981. An illustrated edition of a long poem sequence, *El Inicio*, was published in 1983 (Ayuntamiento Popular de Juchitán). Since then, Volkow has published a travel book, *Viaje a Sur Africa*, and a new collection of poems titled *El Principio*.

EL TEDIO DE EURÍLOCO

"Más allá de la gruta de Caribdis,
más allá de los aullidos de Escila,
hay un punto en que el barco se desploma del océano
y de los que han caído ya ninguno regresa."
Euríloco pensaba sentado en la cubierta
mientras sentía la brisa que hacía ondear las cuerdas
y palpitar las velas como ijares;
miraba aquí y allí, distraído y cansado,
los cabellos de Ulises, las manos de un esclavo
y oía desatento el rechinar de la madera
y el rumor de las voces en esa lengua antigua,
que es hoy una música perdida.
Allí estuvo el mar entre los remos,
transparente y elástico,
pero a los ojos de Euríloco sería
casi invisible de monótono
y la jornada larga, muy tediosa,
y nunca pensó que a cada instante
ese mar evanescente y poderoso
se le alejaba inalcanzable
y era imposible ya el regreso.

THE WEARINESS OF EURYLOCHUS

"Beyond the cavern of Charybdis,
beyond the howl of Scylla,
there is a point where the boat leans from the ocean
and of those who have fallen, none now return."
Eurylochus was thinking, seated on the deck
while he felt the breeze that had been strumming ropes
and urging the sails to quiver like a horse's flanks;
he was watching here and there, absentminded and tired,
Ulysses' hair, the hands of a slave
and he carelessly heard the creaking wood
and the murmur of voices in that ancient tongue
which now is a lost music.
There was the sea between the oars,
transparent and elastic,
but to the eyes of Eurylochus it would be
nearly invisible from monotony
and the long voyage, so tedious,
and he never thought that at each instant
the evanescent and powerful sea
was sliding away, past his reach,
and the return was already impossible.

Translated by Forrest Gander

LA LAVANDERA

Siente ásperas las manos como peces,
ciegos peces que golpean contra la piedra,
incesantes contra la piedra durante años y años;
mira la noche atravesada de ojos,
húmedas miradas deslizantes,
rostros escurridizos, mudos, que se pierden,
miradas de muchachas de piel tersa,
miradas marchitas de las madres cansadas.
El día termina y las gentes regresan a sus casas
y el agua cae del grifo monótona como una canción,
el agua ha perdido la forma de los tubos,
ha perdido la memoria de su cauce en la montaña
y ha construido su camino a golpes,
cercada en sus obstáculos,
como los pies, como los ojos, como las manos.
Mira las sombras que la gente arrastra,
sombras en los muros, las esquinas, las calles,
tintas fugaces que marcan los caminos,
caminos desesperados, afanosos,
que buscan sólo quizá una permanencia.

THE WASHERWOMAN

She feels her hands, scabrous as fish,
blind fish striking against the rock,
incessantly against the rock for years and years;
she watches the night pierced with eyes,
humid, slippery glances,
the mute faces shifting, disappearing,
brilliant glances of girls,
the dazed look of exhausted mothers.
The day ends and people return to their houses
and water runs from the faucet monotonously as a song,
the water has lost the shape of pipes,
lost the memory of its mountain source
and has pounded out its course,
besieged by obstacles
like the feet, like the eyes, like the hands.
She looks at shadows people drag along,
shadows on the walls, corners, the streets,
fugitive ink that marks the beaten roads,
desperate roads, laborious,
looking for only, perhaps, a fidelity.

Translated by Forrest Gander

AUTORRETRATO MUERTA

Los ojos ya no miran
están como ríos muertos,
marchitas las raíces
y yemas de los dedos
donde crecía la tierra
follaje piel adentro.
Desalojaron las sombras
los laberintos del sueño
y enmudeció la oreja
como un pájaro muerto.
El bosque de las venas
fue secando su incendio
y el ovillado viento en los alvéolos
quedóse quieto.
Ya no siente siquiera
el mar que se vacía,
la oscuridad que encierra,
mientras que en otro orbe inconcebible
bajo el agobio inmenso de la noche
se concentra el carbón de las estrellas.

SELF-PORTRAIT, DEAD

Already the eyes aren't watching,
they are like dead rivers,
the roots withered
with the buds of toes
where soil grew
leafy skin inland.
The shadows broke out
from labyrinths of dream
and the ear fell mute
as a dead bird.
The forest of veins
went parching its fire
and the tangled wind in the alveoli
remained quietly.
Already the ocean scarcely feels
it is emptying;
the darkness, that it is locked away,
meanwhile on another inconceivable sphere
under the immense crouch of the night
the coals of stars concentrate.

Translated by Forrest Gander

Desde EL INICIO

I.

El hambre es el primer ojo del cuerpo
el primer ojo en la noche del cuerpo
el ojo con que la carne mira por primera vez la carne

y una sangrienta oscuridad nos enreda hacia dentro

             el ojo
con que te miran mis pies   mis dientes
                mis dedos

             el ojo
con que te miro   como hace siglos
en la noche del tacto
             esa noche
tan parecida a la noche del pez
             del tigre
             de la serpiente
tan parecida a la primera noche de la vida

somos la bestia otra vez al cerrar los ojos
y nuestros cuerpos se abrazan como fauces
              aferrados al sabor de las formas

From EL INICIO

I.

Hunger is the original eye of the body
primeval eye in the dark of the body
the eye with which flesh first beholds flesh

and a sanguinary darkness draws us inward

                    the eye
with which my feet see you   my teeth
                        my fingers

                    the eye
with which I discover you   centuries long
in one night of touching
                        that night
so like the night of the fish
                    the tiger
                    the snake
so like the first night of life

we close our eyes and are beast again
and our bodies are clamped like throats
                        choking on the shapely flavors

VI.

Los amantes
sólo tienen sus manos para amarse
                    sólo tienen sus manos
manos que son pies y alas sobre los cuerpos
manos que buscan incesantes
el animal palpitante de ojos enterrados
dedos que son leños en que los cuerpos se incendian
que son ramas en que florecen las caricias
flores que son aves que son llamas que son manos
manos que se pierden tras su escritura de rayos

manos que recorren la carne de los cuerpos
como estrellas de dedos que en el tacto amanecen
como soles que nacen   como joyas fugaces
como dioses secretos que dibujan la noche

X.

Entre tu cuerpo mi cuerpo
es la huella de tu cuerpo
es el ojo   es el oído de tu cuerpo
                    escucho tus brazos
                          tus dientes
                          tu lengua
                          tus piernas
con toda mi piel escucho la forma de tu cuerpo

entre mi cuerpo tu cuerpo
es otra forma de tu cuerpo
como el agua que es hielo incandescente
o el grifo de la llama en las cosas
                    tu cuerpo
grita en mi cuerpo

VI.

The lovers
have hands solely for loving
                    they have only their hands
hands that are feet and wings over their bodies
hands that constantly seek
the breathing animal behind buried eyes
fingers that set their bodies on fire
that are branches on which caresses flower
flowers that are birds that are flames that are hands
hands that are lost in their lightning writing

hands that travel the flesh of bodies
like stars touching at daybreak
like suns rising   like shooting stars
like secret gods who draw the night

X.

Between your body my body
is the print of your body
is the eye   the sound of your body
                    I hear your forearms
                            your teeth
                            your tongue
                            your thighs
I hear the shape of your body with all my skin

between my body your body
is another form of your body
like water turned to incandescent ice
or the open faucet of flames
                    your body
cries out in my body

            y eres un grito grieta
                un grito astro
un grito mudo   de carne   en mi cuerpo

dime   ¿no es el fuego
la semilla de los mundos distantes
la extraña y súbita forma de su cercanía?

XI.

Estás desnudo
              y tu suavidad es inmensa
tiemblas en mis dedos
tu respiración vuela adentro de tu cuerpo

            eres
como un pájaro en mis manos
            vulnerable
como sólo el deseo podría hacerte vulnerable
ese dolor tan suave con el que nos tocamos
esa entrega en la que conocemos
el abandono de las víctimas

el placer como una fauce
nos lame   nos devora
y nuestros ojos se apagan
              se pierden

 and you, a loosed scream
 a shouted star
a mute cry   of flesh   in my body

tell me   isn't the flame
the seed of distant worlds
the peculiar and sudden nearness of the stars?

XI.

You are nude
and your smoothness is infinite
you tremble to my fingers
your breath flies inside your body

        you are
like a bird in my hands
        vulnerable
as only desire could make you vulnerable
that exquisite pain with which we touch one another
that surrender in which we know
the abandon of victims

pleasure like a tongue
licks us   devours us
and our eyes burn out
        are lost

Translated by Martha Christina

Myriam Moscona

Myriam Moscona was born in Mexico in 1955, the daughter of Jewish Bulgarians who emigrated to America after World War II. She studied journalism and is responsible for a weekly radio program in Mexico City on culture. Besides having written for two journals, *Unomasuno* and *La Jornada*, she has published her poems in numerous magazines and has been included in several anthologies.

In 1983, after receiving a scholarship from the National Institute of Fine Arts, she won an award for young poets and, soon after, published a book of poems, *Ultimo Jardin*. Another collection, *Las Visitantes*, won the 1988 El Premio Aquascalientes award. Her most recent book is *El Arbol de los Nombres* (*Secretaría de Cultura de Jalisco, 1992*).

◆

It is difficult to talk about the work one writes. The only thing I can do is try to describe the theme or themes that have appeared in what I have written: exile, women from outside and within themselves, death from the perspective of the survivors, and in general, the personal or collective sentiment we carry on as human beings. That doesn't say a lot. But about what else have we always spoken?

Desde JARDIN EN TRANCE

II.

No puedo jugar con mi apellido.
Alas me crecen monstruosas.
He de habitar el fango, desperdicios, excrementos.
Tenemos en común pasión por la luz.
Caigo atrapada en el neón encendido.
Ay Venus,
amamos tanto los tiempos ya pasados
que nuestra nostalgia se vuelve una triste forma de adulterio.
Mosconas de nacimiento,
desde Bulgaria vinieron cargando mi destino,
llegaron a depositarme en la ciudad
para después rendirle honor al apellido.
Entre insectos y astros
puede servir de alivio el embrujo de los mares donde me dispongo a caer.
El crepúsculo más lento se avecina.
Ay Venus, ¿qué hacer con este vértigo?
Jinete soy de cien caballos.
Una mujer como yo, se aleja.
Un buque se pierde en altamar.

▼▼

From GARDEN IN PERIL

II.

I cannot fool around with my family name.
Monstrous wings sprout on me.
I must dwell in mud, garbage, dung.
We share a passion for light.
I fall into the burning neon trap.
Ah, Venus,
we love the past so much
that our nostalgia becomes an abject adultery.
Giant flies from birth,
they came from Bulgaria loaded down with my destiny,
they dropped me off securely in the city
that they might honor my name.
Between insects and the stars
I prepare myself to fall into bewitching seas which
            may bring relief.
The slowest sunset draws near.
Ah, Venus, What's to be done with this vertigo?
I am the rider of a hundred horses.
A woman like me, withdraws.
A ship is lost in the high seas.

Translated by C. D. Wright and Lida Aronne-Amestoy

LA MUJER DE LOT NO TIENE NOMBRE

Entonces la mujer de Lot miró atrás,
a espalda de él, y se volvió estatua de sal
—Génesis 19/26

Un giro a la mitad y asestaste al punto.
Todos han muerto, ciertamente.
Tus hijas partieron sin decirte adiós.
Pensaste en tu ciudad,
en los huertos incendiados
que jamás florecerían.

Nadie te liberó.
Tampoco tus ojos encontraron paradero.
No te quedarás sola.
Pájaros nocturnos bajarán,
Lot estará llorando.
Volverá después, te lo aseguro.

Te arrancará el pezón,
le bastará la sola orilla
para sazonar el pan de diez generaciones.

Cada cien años abres tu letargo
apenas logras un lamento:
"Lot, amor mío, tengo enfrente
un espejo que me obliga"

LOT'S WIFE IS NAMELESS

But his wife looked back behind him,
and she became a pillar of salt.
            —Genesis 19:26

A half turn and you took aim.
Surely, all have died.
Your daughters left without saying good-bye.
You thought of your city,
of the scorched orchards
that would never flower.

No one came to rescue you.
Nor did your eyes find a resting place.
You will not be alone.
The night birds will swoop down,
Lot will be weeping.
Afterwards, he will come back. I promise you.

He will tear out your nipple,
its edge alone will be enough for him
to season the bread for ten generations.

Every one hundred years you break through your lethargy
you can barely manage a moan:
"Lot, my love, I have before me
a mirror that holds me."

Cuando levante la gleba
habrá muerto Lot.
Una hoja subirá a coronarse.

Tu saliva será un recuerdo.

When the soil is turned again
Lot will be dead.
A leaf will lift itself up to be crowned.

Your spit will be a memory.

Translated by C. D. Wright and Lida Aronne-Amestoy

LA MUJER DE LOT ENCUENTRA NOMBRE

Caminas
como quien anda el exilio.
"La que vuelve atrás se petrifica".
Una niña
sigue con el dedo el polvo
apilado en la pared.
No quieres dejarla al azar,
pero la muerte
llegará temprano.

Tus hijas escancian el vino que Lot,
seducido por el sopor salado de tu muerte, aceptaría.

La ciudad es tu ascendencia.
No habrá árbol genealógico capaz de marchitarse.
La niña
o la sombra de su ángel
irá a posarse en tu salumbre.

Cargada de tu inmenso velo,
el aire vendrá a permanecer.

Caminas,
con la oración de la mañana entre los labios:
                    nombre de agua
                    soplo

LOT'S WIFE TAKES A NAME

You go forth
as one who walks in exile.
"She who looks back will be petrified."
A girl
draws with her finger in the dust
heaped on the wall.
You don't want to leave her to chance,
but death
will get here early.

Your daughters serve Lot the wine;
seduced by the salty indolence of your death, he would accept.

The city is your heritage.
No family tree can wither.
The girl
or the shadow of her angel
will light on your salt column.

Loaded with your vast veil,
the air will come back to stay.

You go forth,
with the morning prayer between your lips:
                    name of water
                    breath

algún maldito viento que aplacase;
pero Sodoma en llamas muere.

Quiero decirte, Goral,
               la que mira atrás,
               la que habla sola,
               duna, mujer reverso.
Quiero decirte, sodomita,
                         alguien volverá a buscarte.

Domabas la ciudad.
Tu menstruación manchó las calles.

¿Recuerdas la ventana por la que Lot enmudecía?
Los velos en la adolescencia duplican el encanto.

Ahora yaces desnuda, Goral,
mujer de Loto.

Quiero decir,
               alguna vez hembras como tú
giran la mirada para llevarse lo perdido.

Pasaron aves de mal agüero,
luego tu piel,
salada más que el semen,
navío de luz que Lot abordará.

a bad wind that may be appeased;
but Sodom goes up in flames.

I tell you, Goral,
             she who looks back,
             she who speaks alone,
             dune, woman turned backward.
I want to tell you, Sodomite,
                   Someone will come back for you.

You once tamed the city.
Your menstrual flow stained the streets.

Do you remember the window at which Lot always fell mute?
Adolescence doubles the spell of veils.

Now you lie naked, Goral,
Lotus woman.

I mean,
             at times females such as you
glance backwards just to take their losses.

Ill-omened birds have gone by,
then your skin
saltier than semen,
the vessel of light Lot will board.

Translated by C. D. Wright and Lida Aronne-Amestoy

JARDIN DE AUSCHWITZ

Soñe con Auschwitz,
caballos, fogoneros, verdugos y bufones,
        arterias, vapores y calderas.
Soñé toda aquella noche
expediciones al sol con la brújula de Icaro en la piel,
la escalera sin peldaños
es para subir a tomarle medidas al cielo.
El carnaval de antebrazos tendía sus números al viento:
4 56 28 — 4 56 30, fáciles como cualquier teléfono
salvo que morados e indelebles.
Yeguas finas lo portaban en el trasero
¡A lomo
a corso
en cuatro patas!
Todos subían a tomarle medidas al cielo:
hadas, marinos, poetas,
oficiantes del sueño y la parroquia,
condes, sastres, monjas,
profetas y conversos,
toda suerte de aves y reptiles,
guerrilleros, prostitutas.
Todos trepaban aquella gradería.
La muerte caía vertical
mientras ellos se empecinaban en el éxodo.

AUSCHWITZ GARDEN

I dreamed of Auschwitz,
horses, stokers, executioners and buffoons,
          arteries, vapors and caldrons.
I dreamed all night
of expeditions to the sun with the compass of Icarus
          emblazoned on the skin,
the stepless ladder
is there for climbing up to measure the sky.
The carnival of forearms flaunted their digits:
4 56 28 — 4 56 30, easy as phone numbers
but purple and indelible.
Purebred mares wore them on their buttocks,
the post-horse
on its rump,
on all four legs!
Everyone climbed up to measure the sky:
fairies, sailors, poets,
officers of the parish and of sleep,
counts, tailors, nuns,
prophets and converts,
every species of fowl and reptile,
guerrillas, whores.
All of them climbed the steps.
Death fell vertically
while they pressed on with their exodus.

Translated by C. D. Wright and Lida Aronne-Amestoy

JARDIN PERDIDO

Mas los perros estarán fuera;
y los hechiceros, y los disolutos,
y los homicidas y los idólatras
y cualquiera que ama y hace mentira
                    —Apocalipsis, 22/15

¿Hasta cuándo mi espíritu permanecerá
en este marasmo?
                    —Constantino P. Cavafis

Atados a la trenza, dorada como estanque,
caemos sometidos al reflejo.
Por momentos el mundo,
contracorriente de su propio nado,
al centro acerca la visión.
Caleidoscopio quebrado,
salón de espejos cóncavos
donde el ojo contacta con lo inmenso.

De una a otra orilla, andamos con el hato a cuestas.
Negros tulipanes despiden al terruño que alberga sus raíces.
El beso se sueña en el jardín
mientras ambulancias prenden sirenas de mujeres
que perdieron el rostro en las escamas.

El ángel negro

▼▼

LOST GARDEN

But the dogs will be outside;
the sorcerers, and the dissolutes,
and the murderers and the idolators
and everyone who loves lying.
                    —Revelation, 22:15

How long will my soul dwell in
this dullness?
                    —*Constantine P. Cavafy*

We surrender to the reflection,
bound to the blond braid, golden as a pond.
At times the world
flows against its own stroke,
drawing its vision closer to the center.
Fractured kaleidoscope,
parlor of concave mirrors
where the eye touches the infinite.

From one shore to another, we go with the clothes on our back.
Black tulips give up the ground that lodges their roots.
One dreams of kissing in the garden
while ambulances turn on the Sirens
whose faces were lost under scales.

The black angel

partirá las comisuras y saldrá al ras del suelo
a buscar apóstoles que se quieran iniciar.

Estamos hechos a escala del universo.
Fuimos, lo sabes, multitudes
dispersadas por el tiempo.

De sal, los peces excedidos,
sudan el mar que los aturde.
Gitanos perdieron las líneas de la palma.
Heraldos, sacerdotes y alquimistas
saldrán a buscar jardines
que sólo por azar se encuentran.

will part his lips and fly close to the ground
in search of initiates.

We have been made to scale with the galaxy.
We were once, you know, multitudes
dispersed throughout time.

Dredged in salt, the fish
sweat the sea that overwhelmed them.
Gypsies lost the lines of their palms.
Heralds, priests, alchemists
will go forth in search of gardens
that can be found only by chance.

Translated by C. D. Wright
and Lida Aronne-Amestoy

JARDIN DE FIERAS

Eres el innombrable, el ilegal,
el que visita hoteles con florete,
el que perdió la espada
y salió con ella cosida a su victoria.
Se citarán a oscuras,
se besarán menstruando, en los cines,
las tabernas.
Encandilada,
como conejo en medio del camino,
inmóvil—fragmentos antes del desastre—,
el coche con sus faros encendidos, la ciega
y tus ojos la clavan contra el suelo.
¿Qué puedo decirte yo que los observo?
la diosa de la juventud
tiene por collar la adolscencia.

Salvaje es buscar la oscuridad.
El tigre copula de noche, en su jaula,
afilando las espinas de su falo
para clavarlas a laderas espumosas:

Contener el amor lastima el cautiverio.

GARDEN OF BEASTS

You are the unnameable, the illegal,
who visits hotels with a foil,
who lost the sword
and left with her sewn to your victory.
Together you will make a date with the darkness,
will make out menstruating, at the movies,
in bars.
Dazzled,
like a rabbit halfway across the road,
frozen—fractions before the disaster—
the car with its lights ablaze blinds her,
and your eyes pin her to the ground.
What can I tell you, I who see this?
the goddess of youth
has adolescence for a necklace.

Stupid to search for the darkness.
The tiger mates by night, behind bars,
stropping the thorns of his phallus
to penetrate the foaming hillside:

A love held in check salts captivity's sores.

Translated by Forrest Gander

ULTIMO JARDIN

Alabado el jardín de los primeros,
el esplendor perdido, contemplado
por el cíclope de bombas y masacres.

Loor al ángel negro:
último vehículo invocado por el siglo
para volver como locos al primer jardín.

Será el árbol del vicio y del abuso.
No seremos tantos,
será uno solo quien preste su costilla
para crear del último jardín de asfalto
un nuevo jardín de primogénitos.

LAST GARDEN

Praise be the garden of aborigines,
the lost splendor on which
the cyclops of bombs and massacres broods.

Glory to the dark angel:
the last medium invoked by a century
for returning us as lunatics to the first garden.

There will be the tree of depravity and abuse.
We won't be so much;
and then one person will lend his rib
to make the final asphalt garden,
a new-laid garden of forefathers.

Translated by Forrest Gander

Coral Bracho

Coral Bracho was born in Mexico City in 1951. In 1977, she published *Peces de piel fugaz* (Ediciones de La Maquina de Escribir); in 1981 *El ser que va a morir,* her second book, published by Aguascalientes, won the National Poetry Award. *Bajo el destello liquido,* which includes the earlier books, was published in 1988 by Fondo de Cultura Economica. Bracho taught in 1990 at the University of Maryland in College Park. Her poems have appeared in distinguished literary magazines in the United States, Mexico, and Argentina. She is married to the poet Marcelo Uribe.

◆

I can only say that I don't feel comfortable making any statements about my own work. My feeling is that any such statement would implicitly be an evaluation that I think is not up to me to make. Besides that, I think it would also interfere between the reader and the texts and set a limited pattern of approach.

ME REFRACTA A TU VIDA COMO A UN ENIGMA

Como un espejo translúcido
el profundo remanso abierto entre la sombra; lo convexo
a esta sed
de lo que bebo, que palpo como a una esfera en el recinto inextricable,
bajo el destello líquido. Voz

—De entre la danza y el ardor vesperal
Canto sutilísimo   Entre el verde de estupor, de placer
        —Lo que se enciende en la amplitud alta enlaza
en una manera nítida. —Lo que lo cimbra
El viento

y el vellón cenital entre las cuerdas del arpa eolia.
El eucalipto cristalino. Savia
en que se cifra
La calma
y la actitud del agua

De lo que bebo, que aprehendo como un reflejo de ese contacto
        inexpugnable; la claridad
de su raigambre en lo nocturno luminoso, de su bóveda.

Lleno, hondo acorde transparente sobre los bosques como un bramido.

En la oquedad continua del caracol; contra el cristal plomizo
—Tañen

I REFRACT YOUR LIFE LIKE AN ENIGMA

Like a transparent mirror
the deep pool open among shadows; convex
to this thirst
from which I drink, that I touch like a sphere inextricably contained
below the liquid scintillation. Voice

—caught between dance and vesperal warmth
Delicate song   Between the green of stupor, of pleasure
      —which sizzles at high amplitude, engages
with a clear purpose. —What cambers
The wind

and the brassy zenith of aeolic harp strings.
The crystal eucalyptus. Sap
which encodes
The calm
and attitude of water

From what I drink, apprehend like a reflex at that moment of invulnerable
      contact, the clarity
of its rootedness in the luminous night, under its dome.

Full, deep chord transparent over forests like a bellowing.

The shell continues into the coiling socket; against the leaden crystal
—They strum

las lajas de ébano
ante la hoguera que refleja el rastrearse el ulular enardeciente
en los nichos
circulares del canto, el trance—El talismán
        sentido bajo esas termas, de entre esa luz—

Entre los bosques de abedules
como una flama, suaves enjambres. Lo atemporal
entre sus cuerpos encendidos. El sonido
que arraigan (—Los niños trazan su aullido líquido
entre lo ardiente como un espectro vegetal)
Entre los cuencos temporales   El manantial:

Lo que ahí se cimbra.
—Las llamas liban de la noche, entre sus raíces
        sumergidas—Su fluida
redondez,
su acaecer—En lo que bebo, que palpo

slabs of ebony
in front of the blaze that reflects its own traipsing
        the impassioned trill
from the circular nooks of song, the trance—the talisman
        sensed under those thermal springs, in that light—

Among birch forests
like a flame, delicate hives. What's atemporal
among their smoldering bodies. The sound
taking root (—Children trace its swirling howl
through what burns like a vegetal ghost)
In the transitory hollows   The welling spring:

What curves there.
Flames suck from the night, among its submerged roots
        —Its fluid
rotunda,
it's happening—In what I drink, what I touch

Translated by Zoe Anglesey

UNA LUCIÉRNAGA BAJO LA LENGUA

Te Amo desde el sabor inquieto de la fermentación;
en la pulpa festiva. Insectos frescos, azules.
En el zumo reciente, vidriado y dúctil.
Grito que destila la luz:
por las grietas frutales;
bajo el agua musgosa que se adhiere a las sombras. Las papilas, las grutas.
En las tintas herbáceas, instilantes. Desde el tacto azorado. Brillo
que rezuma, agridulce: de los goces feraces,
de los juegos hendidos por la palpitación.
                    Gozne
(Envuelto por el aura nocturna, por los ruidos violáceos,
acendrados, el niño, con la base mullida de su lengua
        expectante, toca,
desde esa tersa, insostenible, lubricidad—lirio
        sensitivo que se pliega a las rocas
si presiente el estigma, el ardor de la luz—la sustancia, la arista
vibrante y fina—en su pétalo absorto, distendido—(joya
que palpita entreabierta; ubres), el ácido
zumo blando (hielo), el marisma,
la savia tierna (cábala), el néctar
        de la luciérnaga).

A LIGHTNING BUG UNDER THE TONGUE

I love you for the nippy taste of fermentation;
in the festive pulp. Insects just hatched, blue.
In the young juice, ductile and glazed.
A scream distills the light:
through the veins of orchard trees
under the mossy water bound to shadows. Papillae, the grottos.
Instilled in herbaceous tones. From the startled touch. Luster
that oozes, bittersweet: from fertile pleasures,
of games split by a heartthrob.
               Hinge
(Swaddled by the nocturnal breeze, by violet-colored sounds,
pure, the child, with the soft undertip of the expectant
     tongue, touches
that glossy, untenable, lubricity—sensitive
      lily that cringes in rocks
if the stigma portends the substance, the glow and shock of light,
vibrant and fine, from its enthralled petal, distended—(jewel
that throbs half-open; udders), the acid
musky juice (frost), the marshiness,
the green sap (cabal), the nectar
      of the lightning bug).

Translated by Zoe Anglesey

TUS LINDES: GRIETAS QUE ME DEVELAN

We must have died alone,
a long long time ago.
                    —*D. B.*

Has pulsado,
has templado mi carne
en tu diafanidad, mis sentidos (hombre de contornos
levísimos, de ojos suaves y limpios);
en la vasta desnudez que derrama,
que desgaja y ofrece;

(Como una esbelta ventana al mar; como el roce delicado,
        insistente, de tu voz).
Las aguas: sendas que te reflejan (celaje inmerso),
        tu afluencia, tus lindes:
grietas que me develan.

—Porque un barniz, una palabra espesa, vivos y muertos,
        una acritud fungosa, de cordajes,
de limo, de carroña frutal, una baba lechosa nos recorre,
        nos pliega, ¿alguien;
alguien hablaba aquí?

Renazco, como un albino, a ese sol:
distancia dolorosa a lo neutro que me mira, que miro.

YOUR BORDERS: CREVICES THAT UNCOVER ME

We must have died alone,
a long long time ago.
                              —D. B.

You have stroked,
you have softened my flesh
in your transparency, my senses (man of fragile
contours, of soft and limpid eyes);
in the vast nudity that overflows,
that dismembers and submits;

(Like a narrow window toward the sea; like the delicate,
        insistent rubbing of your voice).
The waters: paths that reflect you (a submerged canvas of clouds),
        your abundance, your borders:
crevices that uncover me.

—Because a glaze, a dense word, the living and the dead, a fungal
        sourness, of ropes,
of slime, of fruitful carrion, a milky secretion spreads
        over us, contorts us, someone;
was someone speaking here?

I am reborn, like an albino, to that sun:
painful distance toward the neutral one that observes me, that I observe.

Ven, acércate; ven a mirar sus manos, gotas recientes en este fango;
     ven a rodearme.
(Sabor nocturno, fulgor de tierras erguidas, de pasajes sedosos,
     arborescentes, semiocultos;
el mar:

sobre esta playa, entre rumores dispersos y vítreos). Has deslumbrado,
reblandecido

¿En quién revienta esta luz?

—Has forjado, delineado mi cuerpo a tus emanaciones,
a sus trazos escuetos. Has colmado
de raíces, de espacios;
has ahondado, desollado, vuelto vulnerables (porque
     tus yemas tensan
y desprenden,
porque tu luz arranca—gubia suavísima—con su lengua,
     su roce,
mis membranas—en tus aguas; ceiba luminosa
     de espesuras abiertas,
de parajes fluctuantes, excedidos; tu relente)
     mis miembros.

Oye; siente en ese fallo luctuoso, en ese intento segado,
     delicuescente.
¿A quién unge, a quién refracta, a quién desdobla? en su miasma

Miro con ojos sin pigmento ese ruido ceroso
que me es ajeno.

(En mi cuerpo tu piel yergue una selva dúctil
     que fecunda sus bordes;
una pregunta, viña que se interna, que envuelve
     los pasillos rastreados.
—De sus tramas, de sus cimas: la afluencia incontenible.

Come, draw near; come and see his hands, recent drippings in this mire;
 come surround me.
(Evening taste, radiance of proud lands, of silken passages,
 like a tree, half-obscured;
the sea:

on this beach, among scattered murmurs of glass). You have dazzled,
softened

On whom does this light explode?

—You have forged, delineated my body to your emanations,
to their simple outlines. You have overflowed
with roots, with spaces;
you have deepened, flayed, turned vulnerable (because your fingertips
 tighten
and release,
because your light extracts—sweetest gouge—with its tongue,
 its rubbing,
my membranes—in your waters; luminous ceiba
 of accessible thickness,
of alternating places, surpassed; in your evening dew)
 my limbs.

Listen; feel in that mournful decision, in that harvested intent,
 dissolved into water.
Who is anointed, who refracted, who is revealed? in its miasma

I stare with colorless eyes at that waxy noise
that is alien to me.

(In my body your skin arouses a compliant jungle
 that enriches its boundaries;
a question, vineyard that penetrates, that embraces
 the traced passages.
—From their plottings, from their heights: the irresistible richness.

Un cristal que penetra, resinoso, candente, en las vastas
       pupilas ocres
del deseo, las transparenta; un lenguaje minucioso.)
Me has preñado, has urdido entre mi piel;
¿y quién se desplaza aquí?
¿quién desliza por sus dedos?

Bajo esa noche: ¿quién musita entre las tumbas, las zanjas?
Su flama, siempre multiplicada, siempre henchida y secreta,
tus lindes;
Has ahondado, has vertido, me has abierto hasta exhumar;
¿Y quién,
quién lo amortaja aquí?; ¿quién lo estrecha, quién lo besa?
¿Quién lo habita?

A crystal that pierces, resinous, glowing, in the vast
        ocher pupils
of desire, exposes them; a meticulous language.)
You have impregnated me, you have warped my flesh;
and who moves about here?
who slips through their fingers?

Beneath that night: who murmurs among the tombs, the trenches?
Its flame, always multiplied, always swollen and concealed,
your borders;
you have plunged, you have spilled, you have opened me for exhumation;
And who
who enshrouds it here, who tightens it, who kisses it?
Who inhabits it?

Translated by Thomas Hoeksema

SIN TÍTULO

Tu voz (en tu cuerpo los ríos encrespan
un follaje de calma; aguas graves y cadenciosas).

—Desde esta puerta, los goces, sus umbrales;
desde este cerco, se transfiguran—

En tus bosques de arena líquida,
de jade pálido y denso (agua profunda, hendida;
esta puerta labrada en las naves del alba). Me entorno a tu
vertiente—Agua
que se adhiere a la luz (en tu cuerpo los ríos se funden, solidifican
entre las ceibas salitrosas. Llama—puerta de visos ígneos—
que me circundas y trasudas: sobre este vidrio, bajo estos valles
     esponjados, entre esta manta, esta piel

UNTITLED

Your voice (in your body the rivers arouse
a foliage of repose; solemn and rhythmic waters).

—From this door, the pleasures, their thresholds;
from this frame, they are transfigured—

In your forests of liquid sand
of pale, dense jade (deep water, severed;
this door carved on the ships of dawn). I enclose your
fountain—Water
that clings to light (in your body the rivers merge, solidify
among the nitrous ceiba trees. Flame—door of fiery glowing—
you surround and swelter me: above this glass, below these porous
        valleys, between these blankets, this skin

Translated by Thomas Hoeksema

DE SUS OJOS ORNADOS DE ARENAS VÍTREAS

Desde la exhalación de estos peces de mármol,
desde la suavidad sedosa
de sus cantos,
de sus ojos ornados
de arenas vítreas,
la quietud de los templos y los jardines

(en sus sombras de acanto, en las piedras
que tocan y reblandecen)

    han abierto sus lechos,
    han fundado sus cauces
    bajo las hojas tibias de los almendros.

Dicen del tacto
de sus destellos,
de los juegos tranquilos que deslizan al borde,
a la orilla lenta de los ocasos.
De sus labios de hielo.

Ojos de piedras finas.

De la espuma que arrojan, del aroma que vierten

(En los atrios: las velas, los amarantos.)

THEIR DECORATED EYES OF CRYSTALLINE SAND

From the breath of these marble fish,
from the silky smoothness
of their songs,
their decorated eyes
of crystalline sand,
the stillness of the temples and the gardens

(in their acanthus shadows, in the stones
that they touch and soften)

    They have opened their beds
    and established their channels
    beneath the warm leaves of the almond trees.

They speak the touching
of their flashes,
of the peaceful games that flow to the outer edge,
to the lingering margin of the sunsets.
Of their frozen lips.

Eyes of precious stones.

Of the foam they hurl, of the fragrance they spill

(In the courtyards: the candles, the unfaded flowers.)

sobre el ara levísima de las siembras.

> (Desde el templo:
> el perfume de las espigas,
> las escamas,
> los ciervos. Dicen de sus reflejos.)

En las noches,
el mármol frágil de su silencio,
el preciado tatuaje, los trazos limpios

> (han ahogado la luz
> a la orilla; en la arena)

sobre la imagen tersa,
sobre la ofrenda inmóvil
de las praderas.

above the smallest altar of the fields

    (From the temple:
    the perfume of the grains,
    the deer,
    the scales. They speak of their reflections.)

At night
the fragile marble of their silence,
the prized tattoo, the distinctive outlines

    (they have drowned the light
    at the shore; on the sand)

above the polished image,
above the motionless offering
of the meadows.

Translated by Thomas Hoeksema

POBLACIONES LEJANAS

Sus relieves candentes, sus pasajes, son un salmo
luctuoso y monocorde;
los niños corren y gritan,
como pequeños lapsos, en un eterno, enmudecido
sepia demente. Hay ciudades, también,
que dulcifican la luz del sol:
En sus espejos de oro crepuscular las aguas abren y encienden
cercos de aromas y caricias rituales; en sus baños:
las risas, las paredes reverdecientes
—Sus templos beben del mar.

Vagos lindes desiertos (Las caravanas, los vendavales, las
        noches combas y despobladas, las tardes lentas,
son arenas franqueables que las separan) mirajes, ecos que las enturbian,
que las empalman;
un gusto líquido a sal en las furtivas comisuras;
Y esta evocada resonancia.

DISTANT CITIES

Their incandescent reliefs, their passages, they are
a mournful, single-chorded psalm;
the children run squalling
like tiny slips in an endless, hushed
and distracted sepia. There are also cities
that sweeten the sunlight:
In their mirrors of golden gloaming, waters unfold and ignite
pockets of aroma and ritual caresses; in their baths:
laughter, the greening walls;
—Their temples sip from the ocean.

Lovely deserted boundaries (The caravans, foehns, the bulging unmanned
        nights, heavy afternoons,
it is loose sand that holds them apart) mirages, blurring echoes
bind them together;
a liquid taste for salt in the furtive corners;
And this dawning resonance.

Translated by Forrest Gander

▼▼▼

About the Editor . . .

Forrest Gander grew up in Virginia and spent summers in Greenwich Village with his father, who ran a bar on Bleeker Street called The Mod Scene. He studied literature and paleontology and majored in geology at The College of William and Mary, worked for the *Washington Post,* was maimed by cancer. When he recovered, he drove to San Francisco to live in the city where poetry never sleeps.

At San Francisco State University, Gander received an M.A. in English and began his association with the literary book press Lost Roads Publishers. With a grant from the National Endowment for the Arts to publish five books, he and the editor, C. D. Wright, left for Mexico and stayed in Dolores Hidalgo for six months until persistent health problems forced Gander north, where he took cure in the rural Ozarks of Arkansas. While in Dolores Hidalgo, Gander wrote to Octavio Paz for the addresses of some of the striking younger poets *Vuelta* was publishing, and he began collecting names and books in Mexico City. Through the mail, the *Vuelta* list continued to grow and transform. Partly in response to the patriarchal tendencies of the publishing business in Mexico, the time seemed right for an anthology of contemporary Mexican poetry by women.

Forrest Gander's published books of poems include *Rush to the Lake* (Alice James Books), *Eggplants and Lotus Root* (Burning Deck), *Lynchburg* (University of Pittsburgh Press), and *Deeds of Utmost Kindness* (forthcoming from Wesleyan University Press). His long poems have been published in, among other places, *Conjunctions, Sulfur,* and The New Directions anthology. In addition to the anthology *Mouth to Mouth,* Gander has worked with two other American and three Russian poets on a project of collaborative translation called *Wandering Dog.* Gander, an associate professor of English at Providence College, Rhode Island, continues to co-edit Lost Roads Publishers with the poet C. D. Wright.

Mouth to Mouth was designed by R. W. Scholes.
Typestyles are Gill Sans and Perpetua,
designed by Eric Gill.
Typesetting by The Typeworks.
Printed on acid-free Glatfelter
by Princeton University Press.

More Translations from Milkweed Editions:

Amen
Poems by Yehuda Amichai
Translated from the Hebrew
by Yehuda Amichai and Ted Hughes

The Art of Writing
Lu Chi's Wen Fu
Translated from the Chinese
by Sam Hamill

Astonishing World
Selected Poems of Angel Gonzalez
Translated from the Spanish
by Steven Ford Brown

Circe's Mountain
Stories by Marie Luise Kaschnitz
Translated from the German
by Lisel Mueller

Clay and Star
Contemporary Bulgarian Poets
Translated from the Bulgarian and Edited
by Lisa Sapinkopf and Georgi Belev

The House in the Sand
Prose Poems by Pablo Neruda
Translated from the Spanish
by Dennis Maloney and Clark Zlotchew

Trusting Your Life To Water and Eternity
Twenty Poems by Olav H. Hauge
Translated from the Norwegian
by Robert Bly